BASIC
SURVIVAL

International Communication for Professional People

Student's Book

PETER VINEY

MACMILLAN
HEINEMANN
English Language Teaching

Contents Chart

COMMUNICATIONS

BUSINESS

SOCIALIZING

TRAVEL

HOTELS

MONEY

FOOD AND DRINK

COMMUNICATIONS

BUSINESS

SOCIALIZING

TRAVEL

HOTELS

MONEY

FOOD AND DRINK

TOPIC	UNIT	COMMUNICATIVE AIMS	GRAMMAR PRACTICE	VOCABULARY
	17 Introductions	Receiving directions. Introducing yourself. Speaking about mutual acquaintances.	Introduction formulas.	Introductions. Indoor directions.
	18 Itineraries	Getting information from a timetable.	Present continuous formulas. *Going to* future. Present simple (timetable) future.	Days of the week. Dates. Months.
	19 Visitors	Receiving visitors. Offering drinks. Introducing yourself and stating your job.	*Going to do. Would you like … ?* *I'd like …*	Introductions. Drinks. Containers and contents.
	20 Connections	Using communication devices.	Frequency adverbs. *Thank you for (doing).*	Communication devices. Message terms.
	21 Fast Food	Requesting and paying for food.	*Would like.*	Requests. Food. Money.
	22 Gift Store	Shopping for gifts.	Demonstratives (2): *Which one (s)? The (blue) one(s) / How much is it / are they? How old is (he)? What size (is it)?*	Gifts. Colors. Relatives.
	23 Small Talk	Making small talk.	Possessive pronouns (singular). Superlatives: *coldest, wettest, driest.* Asking about opinions: *What do you think of it? / What's it like?/ How do you like (it)?*	Places. Weather.
	24 Car Rental Inquiries	Asking for car rental information.	Prices (per day / per week). *When? What time? Right now /as soon as possible.*	Car grades, makes, and models.
	25 Picking Up a Car	Picking up a rental car. Following instructions.	Present continuous. Requests with *may* and *could.*	Illustrations. Colors.
	26 Routines	Going over a work schedule. Extending an invitation.	Present simple with adverbs of frequency. Sequence words: *first / next / then / finally / after / before.* Invitations: *Would you like to come (with us)?*	Terms of routine. Invitations.
	27 Structures	Understanding a company's hierarchical organization.	*In charge of / responsible for / reports to.*	Job titles.
	28 Lunch	Going to a business lunch.	Suggestions: *Let's … / Why don't we … / How about … ? / What about … ?* Offering to pay: *Let me (pay) / I'll get it / This is on me / I'll pay.*	Invitations. Food.
	29 Dealing With Problems	Dealing with problems.	Offers of help / willingness / requests: all with *'ll / will, it won't stop / work.* Urgency: *immediately / right away / right now / quickly / it's urgent.*	Offers of help. Requests.

COMMUNICATIONS

BUSINESS

SOCIALIZING

TRAVEL

HOTELS

MONEY

FOOD AND DRINK

TOPIC	UNIT	COMMUNICATIVE AIMS	GRAMMAR PRACTICE	VOCABULARY
	30 Arrangements	Making an appointment. Booking a flight.	*Will* future. *Let me see / check.*	Appointments. Flight terms.
	31 Meeting People	Meeting and introducing colleagues.	*I want you to … / I'd like you to …*	Introductions. Forms of address. Names. Job titles.
	32 Traveling in a Group	Organizing group travel.	Giving instructions: *Tell (him) to do it.* Prepositions. *'ll* future. *Probably. Just in case …* Permission: *Is it OK if (I sit up front)?*	Instructions. Directions.
	33 About Yourself	Talking about yourself.	Past tense: *was / were. Last year / for (three) years / months. Where? / What ? / How long?*	Personal, professional history.
	34 Getting Through	Getting through on the telephone.	*When* as connector. Present simple. *I want to do / I want you to do.* Apologies: *I'm afraid … / I'm afraid not …*	Communication terms.
	35 Explaining	Explaining business decisions.	Reasons: *Why? Why not? Because / so. Let me explain …* Connectors: *but, and.*	Descriptions. Reasons.
	36 Punctuation	Writing, dictating, and punctuating a business letter.	Punctuation. Pausing.	Letter-writing formulas.
	37 Polite Inquiries	Making polite inquiries.	Past simple tense with *had / went / was / were.*	Flights. Eating out.
	38 Laundry	Requesting hotel laundry service.	Past simple: *put / left / told / called. Too late.*	Clothes. Laundry service.
	39 Important Messages	Collecting your messages.	Past simple: *came / wrote / gave / looked. Somewhere.*	Messages.
	40 Telephone Services	Directory assistance and other telephone services.	Using phone services.	Countries. Cities. Phone services.
	41 Attractions	Describing city attractions. Describing places / attractions.	*Going to* future.	Locations. Schedules. Days. Dates.
	42 Suggestions	Apologizing for disturbing. Returning a call.	Suggestions and advice: *Why don't you … ? / You should … I'll see you tomorrow / See you then. More / less …* (countable / uncountable)	Apologies. Relations. Gifts. Advice.
	43 The Menu	Ordering a meal.	*I'd like / I'll have / I'll try. What would you like? What do you want? Anything (to drink / for dessert)?*	Food. Countries. States. Nationalities.
	44 At the Table	Receiving food orders. Restaurant etiquette.	Requests / offers. *Could you / Can you / May I … Who?* vs. *Whose?* Possessive adjectives and pronouns: *mine / yours.* Reflexive pronouns: *myself / yourself.*	Stress. Food.

COMMUNICATIONS

BUSINESS

SOCIALIZING

TRAVEL

HOTELS

MONEY

FOOD AND DRINK

TOPIC	UNIT	COMMUNICATIVE AIMS	GRAMMAR PRACTICE	VOCABULARY
	45 Interests	Getting to know someone's interests.	*Like / don't like* + *-ing* forms. *Good at doing / not very good at doing.*	Leisure activities.
	46 E-Mail	Electronic Mail.	Abbreviations. *In / on / at*: days, months, years, times. Rules: do's and don'ts.	E-Mail terms.
	47 Sales Talk	Making a sales pitch for a product.	Present passives: *made in / produced in / bottled in.* Superlatives: *best / biggest.*	Sales terms.
	48 Flightseeing	Talking about vacations.	Past simple for narrative. Regular / irregular verbs. Sequence words.	Descriptions. Outdoor scenery.
	49 Let's Make a Deal	Making a business deal.	*Could / couldn't*: past ability. *More* vs. *less* vs. *fewer.* Comparatives: *bigger / cheaper.*	Apologies. Comparative descriptions.
	50 Gas Station	Returning a rental car. Filling up at a gas station.	*Why … ? Because … You have to …* Abbreviations. *What does this mean? It means …*	Gas station terms. Money. Change.
	51 Checking In	Check in for a flight.	*I'd like … / I can … None / only / nearly / too (late).*	Checking in.
	52 Checking Out	Checking out of a hotel. Using credit cards.	Past tense practice *(did / was / were).* Expressions with *'ll: I hope you'll … / We'll miss you. A / an / some.*	Checking out. Mini-bar items.
	53 Your Cabin	Being shown your room.	*Looking forward to / hope.*	Room facilities. Television facilities.
	54 North to Alaska	Understanding facts and figures.	*Length / area / size / number / height. Two times* (the size of). Superlative form of adjectives.	Geographical facts. Statistics. Natural scenery.
	55 Making Friends	Beginning a conversation. Becoming friends.	*So / so far / then. It tastes (salty). It looks (great).*	Introductions. Small talk.
	56 Computer Problems	Giving advice on computers.	*Should / shouldn't.*	Instructions. Precautions. Computer commands.
	57 Skagway	Sightseeing excursions.	Past tense practice.	Descriptions. Local history.
	58 Souvenirs	Purchasing souvenirs.	*Would like. They're made in (Alaska).*	Shopping. Bargaining terms.
	59 Good News	Receiving good news over the telephone.	*Ask / Tell (him) to … Going to / have to / want to / need to. In (20 minutes) / at (4 o'clock).*	Time phrases. Telephone conversation terms.
	60 Good-Bye	Saying good-bye. Thanking for help.	*Will* future / *going to.* Predicting.	Expressions for saying good-bye.

Introducing the course

These are the main characters in the course. You're going to meet these people in the book. You're going to meet other people too, all of them surviving in English. Good luck!

Her name's Josie Campbell. She's British, but she lives in Vancouver now. She's an excursions manager for Pacific Rim Cruises.

His name's Simon Chang. He's Canadian. He lives in Vancouver and works for Pacific Rim Cruises. He's an assistant in the marketing department.

Her name's Cecilia Grant. She's American. She's from Los Angeles, California. She's the Entertainment Director on the Pacific Rim Voyager.

His name's Kenji Nakamura. He's Japanese-American. He's from San Diego. He's a sports coach. He works for Pacific Rim Cruises.

OSLO
STOCKHOLM
EDINBURGH
MOSCOW
LONDON
WARSAW
BERLIN
PARIS
ROME
MADRID
ATHENS
SEOUL
BEIJING
NEW DELHI
CAIRO
HONG KONG
TAIPEI
BANGKOK
MANILA
LAGOS
KUALA LUMPUR
NAIROBI
SINGAPORE
DJAKARTA
CAPE TOWN
MEL

His name's Edgar Young. He's American, but he works in Vancouver in Canada. He works for AmCan Travel. He's the Sales Director.

Her name's Pearl Li. She's Canadian. She's a reception clerk at the Columbia Towers Hotel in Vancouver.

His name's Jack Hudson. He's American. He lives in Phoenix, Arizona. He works for Absolutely Arizona Mineral Waters. He's a sales representative.

Her name's Alicia Romero. She's American. She's from San Diego, California. She's a photographer. She works for Sagebrush Tours.

ANCHORAGE
SKAGWAY
VANCOUVER
SEATTLE
TORONTO
MONTREAL
DENVER
SAN FRANCISCO
CHICAGO
NEW YORK
LOS ANGELES
SAN DIEGO
HOUSTON
ORLANDO
PHOENIX
MEXICO CITY
CARACAS
BOGOTA
LIMA
SAO PAULO
RIO DE JANEIRO
MONTEVIDEO
SANTIAGO
BUENOS AIRES

Welcome

Welcome to this practical and exciting course for people who need English for work or travel.

This book is based around real-life situations, and along with the cassettes or CDs, gives you everything you need to survive in English. There's a Practice Book too, if you want more written work.

Every page is easy to use and learn from, and gives you important new language which you can read, listen to, practice, and use. You'll be able to make simple everyday conversations, order meals, change travelers checks, check in to a hotel, have meetings, and much, much more!

You can access the book page by page, or dip into it by using the topic symbols to find the situations and language which you need most.

You'll also find helpful grammar reference in the Survival Files at the back; extra communication work through true to life communication activities; and for building vocabulary, there are vocabulary files especially created for your needs and a 400-word wordlist with translations in six languages.

Whether you need English for business trips, vacations, or work with English speakers, this course is right for you!

1 Numbers

Conversation A
Alicia is at San Diego International Airport.

Check-in Clerk: Here's your boarding pass, ma'am. Flight CG 186 to Vancouver. Seat 29K. Gate 11 at two thirty.
Alicia: Thank you very much.

Conversation B
Alicia is on the plane.

Flight Attendant: Good afternoon, ma'am. What's your seat number?
Alicia: Uh, twenty-nine K.
Flight Attendant: That's on the left side of the airplane. It's by the window.
Alicia: Thank you.

Conversation C
Alicia is near her seat.

Alicia: Excuse me. You're in my seat.
Man: Sorry?
Alicia: That's my seat. Twenty-nine K.
Man: This is twenty-eight K.
Alicia: No, it isn't.
Man: Well, where is twenty-eight K?
Alicia: That's twenty-eight K there.
Man: Oh, yes. You're right. It is. Sorry.

1 Listen to Conversations A to C. Complete Alicia's boarding pass.

2 Listen to the recording. Complete the boarding information.

Flight Number ____   Gate Number ____
Seat Number ____   Time ____

3 Alicia is in the departure lounge. Listen to the announcement. Complete the spaces:

a First, passengers in rows ____ through ____
b Next, passengers in rows ____ through ____
c Next, passengers in Business Class, rows ____ through ____
d Finally, passengers in First Class, rows ____ through ____

LANGUAGE BANK		
on the left	in the center	on the right
	straight ahead	
by the window	in the middle	on the aisle

ISSUED BY
CROSS GLOBE AIRWAYS
BOARDING PASS

NAME: ROMERO MS. A

FLIGHT NUMBER:

DESTINATION: VANCOUVER

SEAT NUMBER: GATE NUMBER:

NO SMOKING

BOARDING TIME:

Conversation A
Hiroshi is Japanese. He is on a flight from Tokyo to Vancouver.

Flight Attendant: Salmon, chicken, or vegetarian?
Hiroshi: Chicken, please.
Flight Attendant: Anything to drink?
Hiroshi: Yes. Water, please.
Flight Attendant: Still or sparkling?
Hiroshi: Sorry, I don't understand.
Flight Attendant: This is Evian. It's still. And this is Perrier. It's sparkling.
Hiroshi: Oh, yes. Evian, please.

Conversation B
Alicia is flying from San Diego to Vancouver.

Flight Attendant: Tea or coffee?
Alicia: Coffee, please.
Flight Attendant: Regular or decaffeinated?
Alicia: Regular.
Flight Attendant: Cream and sugar?
Alicia: Cream, please. No sugar.
Flight Attendant: There you go.
Alicia: Thank you.
Flight Attendant: For you, sir?
Man: No, thanks. I'm fine.

1 Complete the notes. Hiroshi is in seat 31C.

> Lunch
> Seat 31 A: Chicken + red wine
> Seat 31 B: Vegetarian meal + white wine
> Seat 31 C:

2 Order a meal and a drink. Use the menu and the pictures.

CROSS GLOBE AIRWAYS
IN-FLIGHT MENU

TOKYO – VANCOUVER

Selection of drinks from the bar:
Water: Still or Sparkling
Soda: Cola, Lemon-Lime, Orange
Wine: Red (California) / White (British Columbia)
✈

Tomato & Mozzarella Cheese Salad
Chicken, Sweet Corn & Rice
or
Salmon, New Potatoes, Peas
or
Vegetarian Lasagne
✈

Chocolate Mousse
✈

Tea or Coffee (regular or decaffeinated)

Conversation A

Josie Campbell is British. She is on an airplane flying from Vancouver to San Diego.

Flight Attendant: Excuse me, ma'am. Are you an American citizen?

Josie: No. No, I'm not.

Flight Attendant: Do you have a visa for the United States?

Josie: Yes, I do.

Flight Attendant: Can you complete this card? It's for immigration.

Josie: All right. Uh, do you have a pen?

Flight Attendant: No, I don't. Sorry.

Conversation B

Josie: Excuse me, do you have a pen?

Edgar: Yes, thank you.

Josie: Uh, can I borrow it?

Edgar: Don't you have one?

Josie: No.

Edgar: Huh … all right. There you go.

Josie: Thank you.

1 📟 **On the airplane there are instructions on video about the immigration form. Listen to the instructions, and complete the U.S. immigration form (I-94) with true information.**

2 ★ **Communication Activities**

Student 1 – use Communication Activities, Section A

Student 2 – use Communication Activities, Section X

Conversation C

Josie: Here's your pen. Thanks.

Edgar: Are you here on vacation?

Josie: No, I'm not. I'm here on business.

Edgar: Are you British?

Josie: Yes, I am, but I work in Vancouver.

Edgar: I work in Vancouver, too.

Josie: Are you Canadian?

Edgar: No, I'm an American citizen.

U.S. Department of Justice
Immigration and Naturalization Service

OMB 1115-0077

Admission Number

Welcome to the United States

954469322 · 03

I-94 Arrival/Departure Record - Instructions

This form must be completed by all persons except U.S. Citizens, returning resident aliens, aliens with immigrant visas, and Canadian Citizens visiting or in transit.

Type or print legibly with pen in ALL CAPITAL LETTERS. Use English. Do not write on the back of this form.

This form is in two parts. Please complete both the Arrival Record (Items 1 through 13) and the Departure Record (Items 14 through 17).

When all items are completed, present this form to the U.S. Immigration and Naturalization Service Inspector.

Item 7 - If you are entering the United States by land, enter **LAND** in this space. If you are entering the United States by ship, enter **SEA** in this space.

Form I-94 (04-15-86)Y

Admission Number

954469322 03

Immigration and
Naturalization Service

I-94
Arrival Record

1. Family Name	
2. First (Given) Name	3. Birth Date (Day/Mo/Yr)
4. Country of Citizenship	5. Sex (Male or Female)
6. Passport Number	7. Airline and Flight Number
8. Country Where You Live	9. City Where You Boarded
10. City Where Visa Was Issued	11. Date Issued (Day/Mo/Yr)
12. Address While in the United States (Number and Street)	
13. City and State	

Departure Number

954469322 03

Immigration and
Naturalization Service

I-94
Departure Record

Conversation A
Immigration control in San Diego, California.

Guard: Step this way. Please stand behind the yellow line … Please stand behind the yellow line … go ahead, ma'am. Booth four … Step this way …

Immigration: Good afternoon, ma'am. Your passport, please.

Josie: There you go.

Immigration: Thank you … that's it. Welcome to the United States, and enjoy your stay.

Josie: Thank you.

Conversation B

Guard: Please pick up your bags, and walk through to Customs control … Please pick up your bags, and walk through to customs control …

Customs: Welcome to the United States. Where are you traveling from?

Josie: I'm traveling from Vancouver.

Customs: Are you British?

Josie: Yes, I am.

Customs: My grandfather's British! He was born in York. Do you know York?

Josie: Yes, I do. It's a lovely city.

Customs: Do you have any prohibited items?

Josie: No, I don't.

Customs: OK. Enjoy your stay here.

Josie: Thank you.

1 🔉 **Listen to conversations A and B. Number the instructions in the correct order from 1 to 5.**

2 ☐ Go to Booth four.
3 ☐ Show your passport.
1 ☐ Stand behind the yellow line.
5 ☐ Walk through to customs control.
4 ☐ Pick up your bags.

2 Look at Suzanna's family tree. Refer to the countries and nationalities vocabulary file at the back of the book. Make sentences about her relatives, e.g.

Frankie's her grandfather.
He's Italian-American.
He was born in Italy.

| Frankie Rossi (grandfather) *(born in Italy – Milan)* | = | Ingrid Svenson (grandmother) *(born in Sweden – Stockholm)* | Jakob Berger (grandfather) *(born in Germany – Frankfurt)* | = | Maria Suarez (grandmother) *(born in Mexico – Monterey)* |

Anna Rossi (mother)
(born in New York City)
=
Paul-Henry Berger (father)
(born in Los Angeles)

Suzanna Berger
(born in San Francisco)

5 Baggage in Hall

The Baggage Hall at Vancouver International Airport. Alicia's waiting at carousel one.

Alicia: Pardon me …

Jack: Yes?

Alicia: That's my bag over there, and I can't reach it.

Jack: Which one? This one?

Alicia: No, not that one. The red one.

Jack: Phew! There you go. It's heavy!

Alicia: Oh, and those are my suitcases too.

Jack: Which ones?

Alicia: Those two blue ones and that aluminum one.

Jack: I can't reach them … just a minute.

Alicia: Please be careful! Don't stand on the carousel.

Jack: Don't worry, ma'am. I'm OK. I can get them.

Alicia: Oh, dear. Are you all right?

Jack: Uh, sure. Are these your suitcases?

Alicia: Well, no. They aren't. Sorry!

1 Make more conversations with the words in the Language Bank. Use the highlighted text as a model.

LANGUAGE BANK		
this	red	bag
that	blue	hard case
these	green	soft case
those	yellow	metal case
	black	backpack
	white	vanity box
	brown	suitcase
	gray	
	silver	

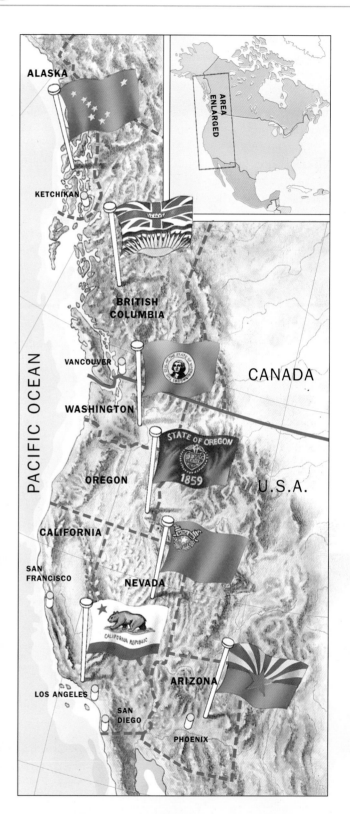

2 U.S. states and Canadian provinces have their own flags. What colors are they?

3 PAIR WORK Look at units 1 to 5. Ask questions about the pictures, e.g.

What color is (it) / are (they)?

5

6 A Ride Downtown

Conversation A
Alicia is at the tourist information booth at Vancouver International Airport.

Alicia: Excuse me …
Clerk: Can I help you, ma'am?
Alicia: Is there a shuttle bus to downtown Vancouver?
Clerk: Sure. Just go right through those doors. The Airport Express stop is right outside.
Alicia: How much is it?
Clerk: $8.50.
Alicia: Hmm. I have a lot of baggage. How much is a taxi?
Clerk: How many bags do you have?
Alicia: Four.
Clerk: How many people are there in your party?
Alicia: Just me. I'm traveling alone.
Clerk: Well, a taxi is around $25.
Alicia: OK. Thank you.
Clerk: You're welcome.

Conversation B
Clerk: Can I help you, sir?
Hiroshi: Yes. Where can I get a taxi downtown?
Clerk: Right outside the terminal. Just follow the signs.
Hiroshi: Thank you.

Conversation C
Alicia: Excuse me …
Hiroshi: Yes?
Alicia: I'm taking a cab downtown, too. Do you want to share the ride?
Hiroshi: Sorry? I don't understand. What do you mean?
Alicia: We can take a cab and split the fare.
Hiroshi: What does 'split the fare' mean?
Alicia: Well, I can pay half the cab fare, and you can pay the other half … fifty / fifty.
Hiroshi: That's a great idea. Thank you.

TRANSPORT TO DOWNTOWN VANCOUVER

- Airport Express – shuttle bus to major downtown hotels. Every 30 minutes. Cost: $8.50 per person.

- Taxi – cabs to the downtown area are around $22 to $25 on the meter. (More in heavy traffic.) This is cheaper if there are three or four people in your party.

- Airport Limousine – Airlimo has a 24-hour service to and from the airport. Flat rate of $26 to downtown area.

- Public transit buses – take the #100 Port Coquitlam Centre / New Westminster Station bus, and transfer at 70th Street to the #20 Victoria route. $1.25 to $2.50 per person.

1 PAIR WORK There are some difficult words highlighted in blue above.

Student 1 – ask your partner what they mean
Student 2 – the answers are in Communication Activities, Section M

2 Ask and answer.

a How much is the Airport Express bus / a taxi / a limo / a public transit bus?
b How much is the Airport Express bus for four people?
c How often do the buses leave?
d Can you get a limo at night?
e How many bags does Alicia have?
f How many people are in her party?
g How much is half the cab fare?

7 Arriving at a Hotel

Conversation A
Vancouver: Alicia is checking in. Pearl Li is at reception.

Pearl: Good evening, ma'am.
Alicia: Good evening. I want to check in.
Pearl: Do you have a reservation?
Alicia: Yes, I do.
Pearl: What name?
Alicia: Romero. Alicia Romero.
Pearl: Just a moment … I don't have your name on the computer.
Alicia: Try my company. That's Sagebrush Tours.
Pearl: Ah, yes. I have it here. Sagebrush Tours, 1276 Market Street, San Diego. Ms. Romero. A single room for five nights.
Alicia: That's right.

Pearl: And the room's reserved on your Visa card. Are you paying with that card?
Alicia: Yes, I am.
Pearl: OK. I just need you to complete this registration card.
Alicia: Thank you. Uh, sorry, what's the date today?
Pearl: May 23rd. You're in room 1631.

Conversation B
San Diego: Edgar Young is checking in.

Edgar: Do you have a room for three nights?
Reception Clerk: Do you have a reservation?
Edgar: No, I don't.
Reception Clerk: I'm sorry, sir. We're nearly full.
Edgar: You don't have a room, then?
Reception Clerk: Well, we have a small room. It's at the back, right over the kitchen …

1 🔊 **Listen to Edgar's conversation at the hotel, and check (✔) the boxes. What facilities does Edgar's room have?**

Facility	Yes	No		Yes	No
King-size bed	☐	☐	In-room movies	☐	☐
Bath	☐	☐	Room safe	☐	☐
Shower	☐	☐	Mini-bar	☐	☐
TV	☐	☐			

2 ★ **Communication Activities**
Student 1 – use Section J
Student 2 – use Section W

3 **Work with a different student. Ask and answer about the completed registration cards from exercise 2, e.g.**

What's (his) family name?

7

8 Elevators

Jack Hudson is in the lobby of the Columbia Towers Hotel. He's there on business.

Lobby

Jack: Pardon me …
Bellman: Yes, sir?
Jack: Which floor is the hotel administration?
Bellman: The third.
Jack: Thanks. Where are the elevators?
Bellman: Over there. Right across the lobby.
Jack: Wait! Hold the elevator!

1 Ask and answer about the hotel, e.g.

Where are the stores?
They're on the mezzanine floor.
Where's the conference center?
It's on the fourth floor.

2 Which of these things do you do in an elevator?

a Hold the door for people
b Press the floor button for people
c Say "Hello"
d Have a conversation
e Tell jokes
f Shake hands with everyone
g Talk about the weather

1st Man: There you go.
Jack: Are you going up?
1st Man: No. I'm going down to the parking level.

Parking level

Woman: Hi.
Jack: Hi. Which floor?
Woman: The rooftop pool. That's the twenty-fifth.
Jack: There you go. Phew. It's a high-speed elevator. We're past my floor already!
Woman: Oh, dear. Sorry.

25th floor

2nd Man: Hold on!
Jack: It's all right. I have the door-hold button.
2nd Man: Thank you.
Jack: Where are you going?
2nd Man: The twenty-first. Thanks.

21st floor

Jack: Which floor do you want?
3rd Man: The second. Thank you.
Jack: You're welcome.
3rd Man: Are you the elevator operator?
Jack: Me? No. No, I'm not the elevator operator. I'm just here on business.

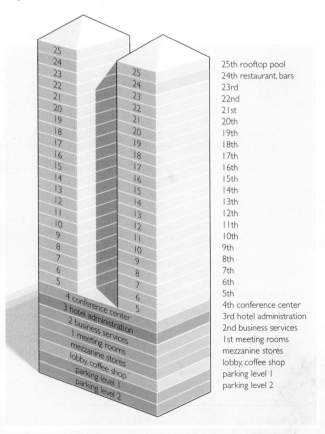

25th rooftop pool
24th restaurant, bars
23rd
22nd
21st
20th
19th
18th
17th
16th
15th
14th
13th
12th
11th
10th
9th
8th
7th
6th
5th
4th conference center
3rd hotel administration
2nd business services
1st meeting rooms
mezzanine stores
lobby, coffee shop
parking level 1
parking level 2

9 An Appointment

Conversation A
The hotel administration department.

Jack: Good morning! And how are you today?

Secretary: Good morning. How can I help you?

Jack: Jack Hudson. Absolutely Arizona Mineral Waters. Here's my card. Can I see the manager?

Secretary: The catering manager?

Jack: Yes, is he in?

Secretary: <u>Ms.</u> Alvarez is in. Is she expecting you?

Jack: Uh, no, she isn't.

Secretary: So you don't have an appointment.

Jack: No, I don't, but …

Secretary: Ms. Alvarez is in a meeting.

Jack: I can wait …

Secretary: Sorry. She has appointments all day.

Conversation B

Jack: Can I make an appointment for tomorrow, please?

Secretary: She has her appointment book with her. Can I call you later?

Jack: Uh, sure. You can leave a message at my hotel.

Secretary: Where are you staying?

Jack: I'm staying at the Pioneer Hotel on Granville Street.

Secretary: So you aren't staying here?

Jack: Here? On my expense account? Are you kidding?

Secretary: OK, Mr. Hudson. Is any time tomorrow OK?

Jack: Sure. Yes. Any time's OK.

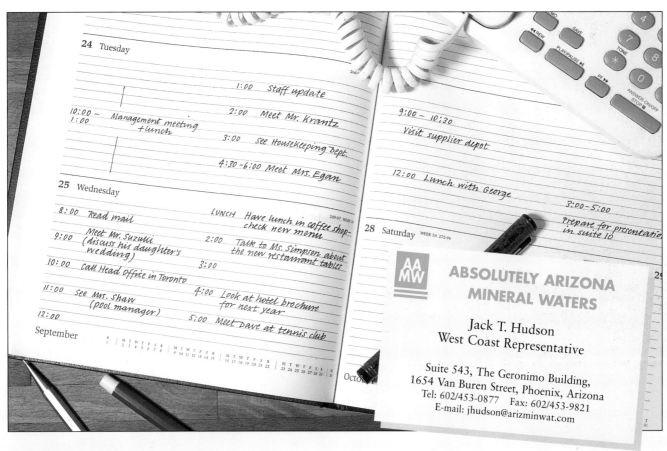

1 Ask and answer.

a Does Jack know the catering manager?

b Does the catering manager know him?

c Is she expecting him?

d Does he have an appointment?

e Does she have any appointments today?

f Does the secretary have Ms. Alvarez's appointment book?

g Who has it?

h Is Jack staying at the Columbia Towers?

i Does Jack have a large expense account?

j Where is he staying?

k Is the Pioneer an expensive hotel?

l Is the Columbia Towers an expensive hotel?

2 This is a page from Ms. Alvarez's appointment book. When can she see Jack Hudson tomorrow? Ask and answer about her day, e.g.

What is she doing at 8 o'clock?

10 Breakfast Buffet

Conversation A
Edgar's in his hotel in San Diego.

Edgar: Good morning.
Host: Good morning, sir. Table for one?
Edgar: Please.
Host: Smoking or non-smoking?
Edgar: Non-smoking.
Host: Right this way.

Conversation B

Waiter: Good morning. I'm Juan, and I'm your waiter for today. Tea or coffee?
Edgar: Coffee, please.
Waiter: Can I recommend our buffet? That's $12.95. Coffee's included.

Edgar: Yes, that's fine. The buffet.
Waiter: It's right over there. Help yourself, and enjoy your breakfast.

Conversation C

Edgar: Excuse me, is there any more milk?
Waiter: Sure there is. Coming right up.
Edgar: Cornflakes … Cheerios … Granola. No. Are there any Rice Krispies?
Waiter: Aren't there any in the bowl?
Edgar: No, there aren't.
Waiter: Then we don't have any Rice Krispies.
Edgar: No Rice Krispies! I don't believe it!
Waiter: Sorry. But it _is_ nine thirty. We serve breakfast from seven.

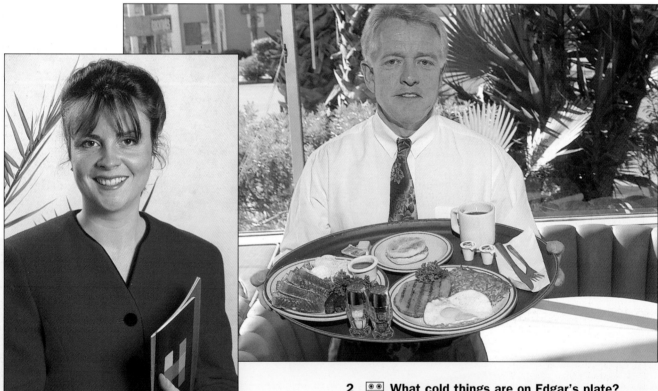

1 👓 **What hot food is on Edgar's plate?**
Listen and check (✔) the boxes.

- ☐ bacon
- ☐ fried potatoes
- ☐ hash browns
- ☐ mushrooms
- ☐ tomatoes
- ☐ English muffins
- ☐ scrambled eggs
- ☐ fried eggs
- ☐ boiled eggs
- ☐ poached eggs
- ☐ sausages
- ☐ French toast

2 👓 **What cold things are on Edgar's plate?**
Listen and check (✔) the boxes.

- ☐ ketchup
- ☐ barbecue sauce
- ☐ maple syrup
- ☐ breakfast rolls
- ☐ salt
- ☐ pepper
- ☐ French mustard
- ☐ milk

3 Ask questions about Edgar's breakfast plate, e.g.

Is there any ketchup?
No, there isn't. / Yes, there is.
Are there any fried eggs?
No, there aren't. / Yes, there are.

4 Ask questions about the buffet.

11 Hotel Reception

Conversation A
Pearl Li is the reception clerk at the Columbia Towers Hotel in Vancouver.

Alicia: Can you mail these for me?

Pearl: Sure. Where to?

Alicia: Uh, one to France, two to San Diego, and one to Toronto, please.

Pearl: The international postcard rate is 90¢, U.S.A. is 52¢, and Canada is 45¢. That's $2.39.

Alicia: Here's two fifty.

Pearl: Thank you. That's eleven cents change.

Conversation B

Woman: Can I leave a message for Mr. Alain Charest? He's a guest here.

Pearl: Sure, do you know his room number?

Woman: Uh, no, I don't.

Pearl: That's OK. I can find it.

Conversation C

Alain: Good morning. Are there any messages for me? Alain Charest. Room 1132.

Pearl: 1132? Yes, there's one. Here you are.

Alain: Thanks. And can you fax this for me?

Pearl: Two pages, to Montreal, 514-087-9321.

Alain: That's right. Can you charge it to my room?

Pearl: Of course, Mr. Charest.

1 Look at Conversation A. Make conversations with this information:

Canadian postcard postal rates:
Canada: 55 cents
U.S.A., Mexico: 60 cents
International (outside North America): 85 cents

Use these places:

Canada: Montreal, Ottawa, Calgary, Quebec
U.S.A.: Dallas, Boston, Miami, Chicago
International: Brazil, Japan, The U.K., Korea

2 Write a postcard to a friend. Write the address and a short message.

3 Look at Conversation B. Make conversations with this information:

Alicia Romero / she / her room number
Mr. and Mrs. Steinway / they / their room number

4 Look at Conversation C. Make conversations with this information:

Mr. and Mrs. Steinway / room 1819 / for us
4 pages / New York / 212-974-4437

12 City Guide

CITY GUIDE TO ... VANCOUVER

The City of Vancouver, in the province of British Columbia, is only just over 100 years old (1886). The population of British Columbia is 2.5 million, and more than half lives in Greater Vancouver. It is the third largest city in Canada. It has a beautiful location with water on three sides. Vancouver has a mild climate. You can get to the ocean, the beach, or the mountains very quickly. It is only 25 miles from the border with the U.S.A. Vancouver is a major North-American port (the second largest in America). It's the largest port on the West Coast. It's also a major center of tourism. The most famous building is Canada Place (1986). Canada Place is the terminal for cruise ships to Alaska.

1 Write a similar text about San Diego. Use this information:

San Diego / state / California
more than 220 years old (1769)
population 2.5 million
2nd city / California
dry, sunny climate
ocean, mountains, desert
San Diego Zoo – largest in world
18 miles / Mexico
tourism 3rd largest industry (1st = manufacturing, 2nd = U.S. military)
building – Mission San Diego de Alcalá (1769)

2 Talk about your town. Ask and answer.

What's your home town?
Do you live there now?
What state / province is it in?
Is it the largest city in the state / province?
What's the population?
What's the climate like?
Is it mild / hot / dry / wet / cold?
Is it near the mountains / desert / a river?
Is it far from the border with another country?
Is it a center of tourism?
What industries are there?
What's the most famous building?

13 Concierge Desk

Peter Grotowski works on the concierge desk at the Columbia Towers.

Alicia: Good morning. I'm going to the cruise ship terminal. Do I need a taxi?

Peter: Canada Place? No, ma'am. You can walk. It's not far. It's only about a five-minute walk.

Alicia: Fine. Which way is it?

Peter: Here's a map. We're right here. Turn right outside the hotel, and walk down Granville Street for about three blocks. The Canadian Pacific Station is at the end of the street. Take a left, then a right. You can't miss it. It's right in front of you.

Alicia: Thanks. Can I take the map?

Peter: Sure.

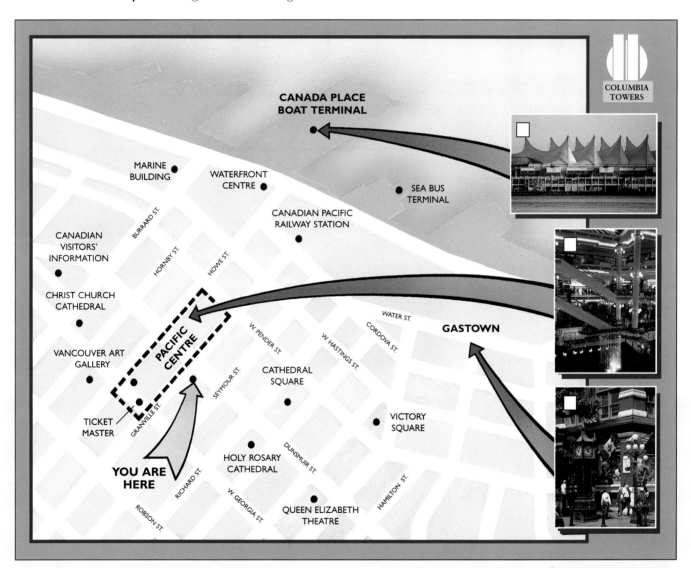

1. 🎧 **Listen to the three conversations. Mark the routes and the destinations on the map. Write 1, 2, 3.**

2. **Give directions from the hotel to these places:**

    Gastown   Christ Church Cathedral
    Victory Square   The Seabus Terminal

    To the right there are four groups of directions. Which can you use for each of the places above?

---

about three blocks go through the station follow the signs	a ten-minute walk can go different ways opposite Canada Place
a five-minute walk go past the cathedral It's on your left	go toward the waterfront turn left at the station take the left fork

3. **PAIR WORK Choose a location. Give directions from the hotel to the location.**

13

Edgar Young is in the hallway of the Quantity Inn hotel in San Diego.

Edgar: Come on!

Housekeeper: Is there a problem, sir? Please don't hit the machine again.

Edgar: But this machine isn't working! My money's in the machine, and so is my candy bar!

Housekeeper: Press 'reject coins'. There you go. Four quarters, two dimes, and a nickel. The machine only takes quarters.

Edgar: Do you have a quarter?

Housekeeper: Sure. There you go.

Edgar: What about my candy bar!

Housekeeper: Don't worry. Put the coins in the slot.

Edgar: But it isn't working.

Housekeeper: Put them in, then select the candy. What do you want?

Edgar: A chocolate bar.

Housekeeper: OK. Chocolate bar. That's …C4. Press C then 4. There you go.

Edgar: Thanks.

Housekeeper: You're welcome.

Edgar: Hey! This is a nut chocolate bar! I don't like nuts!

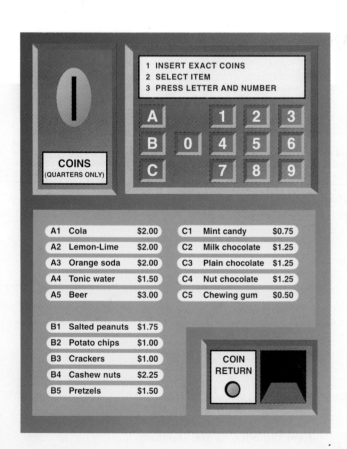

1 **INSERT EXACT COINS**
2 **SELECT ITEM**
3 **PRESS LETTER AND NUMBER**

A   1 2 3
B 0 4 5 6
C   7 8 9

COINS (QUARTERS ONLY)

A1	Cola	$2.00
A2	Lemon-Lime	$2.00
A3	Orange soda	$2.00
A4	Tonic water	$1.50
A5	Beer	$3.00

B1	Salted peanuts	$1.75
B2	Potato chips	$1.00
B3	Crackers	$1.00
B4	Cashew nuts	$2.25
B5	Pretzels	$1.50

C1	Mint candy	$0.75
C2	Milk chocolate	$1.25
C3	Plain chocolate	$1.25
C4	Nut chocolate	$1.25
C5	Chewing gum	$0.50

COIN RETURN

1 **Make more conversations with the information on the vending machine.**

2 **Look at these instructions for a VCR timer. Put them in the correct order.**

☐ Finally press "Timer record".
☐ Next select "Finish time".
☐ Then select day. Press the button until the display indicates the correct date (1 to 31).
☐ First select the program number (1 to 99).
☐ Then select "Start time".
☐ Next select hour. Use the 24-hour clock (i.e. 8 o'clock = 20:00).
☐ Select minutes (00 to 59).
☐ Select hours again, (00 to 23:00) then minutes again (00 to 59).

3 **Give instructions for one of these things:**

How to make coffee
How to make tea
How to play Track 6 on a CD

15 Wrong Number

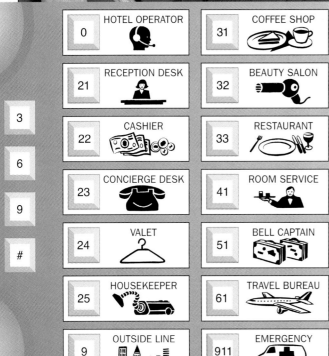

Conversation A

Edgar is in his room. He wants to make a call.

Edgar: 321-7844 …

Voice: Beauty Salon. This is Tania. May I help you?

Edgar: Sorry. Can you repeat that?

Voice: Beauty Salon. This is Tania. May I help you?

Edgar: I don't want the Beauty Salon! Is this 321-7844?

Voice: Are you calling from inside the hotel?

Edgar: Yes.

Voice: And do you want an outside line?

Edgar: Of course I want an outside line!

Voice: This is 32. It's an internal number. Press 9 before the number for an outside line.

Conversation B

Edgar: OK. 9-321-7844.

Voice: Hello?

Edgar: May I speak to Ms. Lowe, please?

Voice: Who?

Edgar: Ms. Lowe.

Voice: Who is this?

Edgar: This is Edgar Young. AmCan. I'm in …

Voice: What number are you calling?

Edgar: 321-7844.

Voice: I'm sorry. You have the wrong number.

Edgar: Oh! Sorry to disturb you.

Voice: That's OK.

2 Which internal number does Edgar press for these inquiries?

  a He wants a sandwich and coffee.

  b He has some dirty laundry.

  c He wants an airline ticket.

  d He has a problem with his shower.

  e He wants the police.

  f He wants a haircut.

  g He wants a dinner reservation.

  h He wants the exchange rate for Canadian dollars into U.S. dollars.

3 Look at Conversation B. Make conversations with this information:

- Mr. Gatsby / 408-7513
- Mrs. Wharton / 711-6375
- Ms. Stein / 401-7499
- Mr. Hemingway / 857-0033
- Miss Buck / 364-6605
- Dr. Williams / 212-5088

1 Look at Conversation A, and make more conversations.

16 A Taxi Ride

Conversation A

Josie Campbell is outside her hotel.

Doorman: Are you checking out, ma'am?
Josie: Yes.
Doorman: Taxi?
Josie: Please.
Doorman: Where are you heading?
Josie: Downtown.

Conversation B

Driver: Where to?
Josie: Pier B, on Harbor Drive.
Driver: OK. Are you going on a cruise?
Josie: I work on a ship. The *Pacific Rim Voyager*.
Driver: Oh, right. So you're a sailor, huh?
Josie: No, I'm not a sailor!
Driver: What do you do?
Josie: I'm the excursions manager.

Conversation C

Driver: This is it. That's $8.50.
Josie: Thanks. There you go.
Driver: Out of twenty … that's $11.50 change.
Josie: Just give me $10.
Driver: Thank you. Have a good trip.

U.S. Money

dollar = 100 cents	bills – $1, $5, $10, $20, $50, $100
quarter = 25 cents	coins – 1¢, 5¢, 10¢, 25¢
dime = 10 cents	
nickel = 5 cents	
penny = 1 cent	

---

1 Look at Conversation B. Make conversations with this information:

Sea World / on Mission Bay
Here on vacation?
No. Work at Sea World.
Tour guide?
No. Dolphin trainer.

Globe Theater / Balboa Park
Going to see a play?
No. Work there.
Actor?
No. Director.

2 U.S. money: fill in the blanks, e.g.

$2.26 = Two dollars twenty-six
A quarter and a nickel = thirty cents

a Three quarters, a dime, and two cents =
b Four nickels and a dime =
c A five dollar bill, four quarters, and a cent =
d A ten dollar bill, a quarter, and two dimes =
e Four cents, a nickel, and a quarter =
f A twenty, a dollar, and three nickels =

3 Look at Conversation C, and make more conversations.

Fare: thirty-four dollars
You have: two twenty-dollar bills

Fare: Seventeen dollars
You have: a twenty-dollar bill

17 Introductions

Conversation A
Josie is on board the *Pacific Rim Voyager*.
She's meeting her new boss for the first time.

Sailor: Good morning. How may I help you?
Josie: Hi. I'm looking for Ms. Grant's office.
Sailor: Ms. Grant? Her office is straight along the hallway on the left. It's number 104. Her name's on the door.
Josie: Thank you.
Sailor: You're welcome.

Conversation B

Josie: Good morning … Ms. Grant?
Cecilia: I'm Cecilia Grant. How may I help you?
Josie: How do you do. I'm Josie Campbell. I'm the new excursions manager.
Cecilia: Pleased to meet you, Josie. Take a seat.
Josie: Thank you, Ms. Grant.

Conversation C

Cecilia: Please call me Cecilia.
Josie: OK … Cecilia. So, you're the entertainment director.
Cecilia: That's right. Welcome aboard the *Voyager*!
Josie: Thank you. It's good to be here.
Cecilia: You're from the *Pacific Rim Traveler*. Do you know Philip Van Dorn?

Josie: Of course. He's the First Officer.
Cecilia: He's a good friend of mine. Say, come and see your new office. It's right next door.
Josie: Thank you.

---

1 **PAIR WORK You're on the stairs. Ask for directions to the places on the diagram.**

102	103	104	105	106	107
THEATER MANAGER	REST ROOM	MS. GRANT ENTERTAINMENT DIRECTOR	EXCURSIONS MANAGER	SPORTS MANAGER	HEALTH CLUB MANAGER

112	113	STAIRS	114	115
COPY ROOM	PERSONNEL MANAGER		CATERING DIRECTOR	BARS MANAGER

DECK 2: SHIP ADMINISTRATION OFFICES

2 **Match the sentences:**

Greeting	Response
Hello.	OK … Tom.
How do you do?	I'm glad to be here.
Please call me Tom.	Thank you.
Welcome to Smith Inc.	Fine, thanks. And you?
So, you're the director.	That's right.
Please sit down.	Hello.

3 **Put the sentences below in the correct order, then practice the conversation.**

B: Thank you.
B: Of course. She works in the Data Processing department.
A: She's an old friend of mine.
B: That's correct.
A: You're from the London office, aren't you?
A: Do you know Cathy Stokes?
B: Oh, really?
A: Please have a seat.

Now make conversations with this information:

New York office / Gloria Manuel / Computer Department
Washington factory / Steve Chang / Quality Control department

17

18 Itineraries

Josie Campbell is asking Cecilia about the itinerary of the _Pacific Rim Voyager._

Josie: Where are we going on Wednesday?
Cecilia: Wednesday. Is that May the 30th?
Josie: Yes, that's right.
Cecilia: We're going to Monterey.

Josie: What time do we arrive there?
Cecilia: At 8 a.m.
Josie: And what time do we leave?
Cecilia: At 5 p.m.

ITINERARY CRUISE 619
7 DAYS PACIFIC COAST HIGHLIGHTS
San Diego – Vancouver

DATE	DAY	VOYAGER	ARRIVE/DEPART
May 28	Monday	San Diego, California	Depart 10 a.m.
		Cruising the Pacific	
May 29	Tuesday	Catalina Island	8 a.m. / 11 a.m.
		Santa Barbara	3 p.m. / 8 p.m.
May 30	Wednesday	Monterey, California	8 a.m. / 5 p.m.
May 31	Thursday	San Francisco	7 a.m. / 6 p.m.
June 1	Friday	Eureka, California	8 a.m. / 1 p.m.
		Cruising the Pacific	
June 2	Saturday	Cruising the Pacific	
June 3	Sunday	Vancouver, B.C.	Arrive 10 a.m.

1 Ask and answer.

   a When are they going to Monterey?
   b Does the ship arrive there at 7 a.m.?
   c What time does it arrive?
   d When does it leave?

Dates

American style (month – day – year):
In the U.S.A. and Canada, 5/12 is May 12th.
Write May 12th. You can also write 12 May in Britain.

International style (day – month – year):
In Britain and in most other countries, 5/12 is December 5th.

We write December 5 or December 5th.
We usually say December <u>the</u> fifth & May <u>the</u> twelfth.

In the U.S.A. you can also say December fifth.

* On U.S. immigration cards, they ask you to write the date in the international style (day – month – year).

2 Make sentences like this:
January is the first month of the year.

Now say these dates in the American style and in the British style.
5/12/95   3/2/67   15/11/96
10/9/99   4/1/86   8/3/70

3 Make more conversations between Josie and Cecilia. Ask and answer, e.g.

   Josie: When are we going to Monterey?
   Cecilia: On Wednesday the thirtieth.

4 ★ Communication Activities
   Student 1 – use Section B
   Student 2 – use Section P

Conversation A
Simon Chang works at the Pacific Rim
Cruises office at Canada Place in Vancouver.

Simon: May I help you?
Alicia: Yes, thank you. I'm Alicia Romero. From Sagebrush Tours, San Diego.
Simon: Oh, right! You're the photographer. It's good to meet you.
Alicia: That's right. I'm the photographer.
Simon: And you're going to take pictures of the Alaska cruise for the brochure.
Alicia: Yes … and I'm going to take some pictures around Vancouver.
Simon: Well, that's great. Take a seat. I'm Simon Chang. I'm Mr. Dawson's assistant. We can talk about the brochure.

Conversation B

Simon: Can I get you something to drink?
Alicia: Uh, yes. Thanks.
Simon: Would you like coffee, tea, or a cold drink?
Alicia: I'd like tea, please.
Simon: With milk or lemon?

1 **Look at the Language Bank. Role-play Conversation A. Replace the highlighted expressions in the conversation.**

2 **We often offer visitors a drink. Use the pictures, and role-play Conversation B with different words.**

Alicia: Lemon, please.
Simon: Sugar?
Alicia: No, thanks.
Simon: OK. Just a minute. Excuse me. I'm going to make the tea. Here's last year's brochure. You can take a look while you're waiting.

3 **Which containers can go with which contents? Draw lines. Can the containers match with more than one word from the contents list?**

container	contents
packet	tea
pot	herb tea
cup	coffee
jug	hot chocolate
pack	milk
spoonful	cream
jar	sugar
can	sweet 'n low

LANGUAGE BANK		
Introduce yourself	**state your job**	**sit down**
I'm Alicia Romero. My name's Alicia Romero.	I'm the photographer. I'm from Sagebrush Tours. I work for Sagebrush Tours.	Take a seat / chair. Please sit down. Would you like to sit down?

Questionnaire

1 Which of these do you use?

☐ a telephone ☐ a pay phone ☐ a mobile phone
☐ a car phone ☐ an answering machine ☐ a fax machine
☐ a modem ☐ a fax modem ☐ a caller display
☐ a video phone ☐ a phone card

2 How many extensions are there ...

☐ at home? ☐ at work?

3 How often do you use the phone?

☐ very often ☐ often ☐ occasionally
☐ once or twice a day ☐ not every day

4 When you hear an answering machine, what do you do?

☐ always leave a message
☐ sometimes leave a message
☐ never leave a message

5 When you don't know a number, what do you prefer to do?

☐ look in a phone directory ☐ call Directory Assistance

---

1 PAIR WORK Interview a partner and complete the questionnaire.

2 ▣▣ Edgar Young is calling from his room in San Diego. Listen to his phone calls.

Call 1, Part 1. Complete the spaces in this transcript:

Thank you for ____ Sagebrush Tours. Your call is in a call-waiting system. Please ____ until one of our telephone operators is ____ .
Thank you for ____ Your call is ____ in a call-waiting system. Please ____ until one of our telephone operators is ____ .

3 ▣▣ Call 1, Part 2. What does the operator say?

a Thank you for (calling / holding / waiting).
b How (can / may) I help you?
c Please (wait / hang on / hold).
d I'm (calling her / trying her extension / connecting you)
Note: all the answers are possible.

4 ▣▣ Call 1, Part 3. Underline the differences in this transcript of Cathy Lowe's message. Then correct them.

Hi there, this is Cathy Lowe. I'm not at work right now. Please give your phone number after the beep, and I'll call you soon.

5 Edgar Young's message is too long for the answering machine. Write a short message. (The phone number of the Quantity Inn is 866-1414. He's in Room 213.)

6 ▣▣ Call 2. Write the numbers in the spaces.

a Press ____ for reservations.
b Press ____ for recorded information.
c Press ____ for brochures.
d Press ____ for other inquiries.

7 Write an answering machine message for yourself.

21 Fast Food

It's eleven thirty. Jack Hudson is at a fast-food outlet in a mall.

Server: Next. Yes, sir?
Jack: I'd like a Big Burger, please.
Server: Big Burger. Anything else?
Jack: Yes. With fries.
Server: Regular or large fries?
Jack: Large.
Server: Anything to drink?
Jack: Yeah, coffee.
Server: Is that everything?
Jack: Yup. That's it.
Server: OK. That's a Big Burger, with large fries, and coffee?
Jack: Right.
Server: That's five fifty-one with the tax.
Jack: There you go.
Server: Out of ten. Four forty-nine change. It's coming right up.

1 Look at the conversation, and make more conversations with the menu.

2 📟 Listen to Jack and the server. Answer the questions:

   a Would he like vanilla or chocolate ice cream?
   b How much is it?
   c What bill does Jack offer the server?
   d Can the server make change?
   e Does Jack have anything smaller?

BIG BURGER WORLD

BIG BURGER 4 oz burger	$2.75
BIG CHEESE 4 oz cheeseburger	$3.25
BACON BURGER 4 oz burger with Canadian bacon	$3.25
BIG DOG hot dog	$1.95
BIG SALAD salad bar	$2.95
NACHOS with HOT CHEESE	$2.25
FRIES regular $1.00	large $1.45
SOFTFREEZE ICE CREAM vanilla, chocolate	$1.70
BIG SHAKE vanilla, strawberry, chocolate	$2.95
BIG COLA regular $0.95	large $1.35
COFFEE, TEA, ICED TEA, LEMON-LIME SODA	$0.95

Recycle it! All Big Burger packaging is recyclable.
All Big Burger meats are from cruelty-free farms.

LANGUAGE BANK

Server:

Do you have	anything smaller? the right money?
Out of twenty?	That's …

Customer:

Sorry, I only have a	(twenty dollar bill).
Sorry, can you change a	(fifty pound note)?

Sorry, I don't have anything smaller.
Can I have (some quarters / dollar coins) in the change?

Taxes

In the U.S.A. and Canada sales tax is added to the price you pay. The tax is different in different states and provinces, e.g. California 8%, British Columbia 7%.

21

22 Gift Store

Conversation A
Hiroshi Tanaka is in the gift store in the lobby of the Columbia Towers Hotel.

Hiroshi: How much is this?
Salesperson: The baseball cap? It's $12.95.
Hiroshi: What size is it?
Salesperson: They're all the same. One size fits all.
Hiroshi: That's OK.

Conversation B
Hiroshi: How much are those T-shirts?
Salesperson: Which ones?
Hiroshi: The dark blue ones.
Salesperson: They're eighteen dollars each.
Hiroshi: What sizes do you have?
Salesperson: Small, medium, large, and extra large. Is it for you?
Hiroshi: No. It's for my son.
Salesperson: How old is he?
Hiroshi: Thirteen.
Salesperson: I suppose medium, then.

Conversation C
Hiroshi: OK. The cap and the T-shirt, then.
Salesperson: That's thirty ninety-five together. Thirty-four twelve with the tax.
Hiroshi: Do you take travelers checks?
Salesperson: Sure. Just sign and date it. I have a stamp with the store name.
Hiroshi: There you go.
Salesperson: That's fifteen eighty-eight change.

---

1 **Underline** all the questions in Conversations A to C. What are the answers?

2 Look at Conversation A. Use the Language Bank and the prices. Ask about prices and sizes, e.g.

How much is this / that?
How much is this / that one?
How much is the blue one?

3 Look at Conversation B. Use the Language Bank and the prices to choose presents for your relatives, e.g.

How much are these / those?
How much are the large ones?
No. It's for my mother.

4 Total your purchases, and pay with a travelers check.

LANGUAGE BANK

More colors

| light gray | dark gray | brown | beige |
| maroon | cream | dark blue | light blue |

Is it for you? No, it's for my ...

| father | daughter | husband | wife |
| mother | brother | sister | son |

baseball cap, $12.95
guide book, $11.75
key ring, $3.50
T-shirts, $18 each
ties, $29.55 each
sweatshirts, $24.95 each
scarves, $10.50 each

23 Small Talk

Conversation A
Alicia and Simon are making small talk or social conversation, before they discuss work.

Simon: There we go. Two teas.
Alicia: Which one's mine?
Simon: That one. The one without a spoon. There's sugar in mine, but there's no sugar in yours.
Alicia: Thanks.
Simon: Be careful, it's hot!

Conversation B

Simon: Is this your first visit to Vancouver?
Alicia: Yes, it is.
Simon: What do you think of it?
Alicia: It's beautiful. Really beautiful.
Simon: I agree, but then it's my home town!
Alicia: You're very lucky.

Conversation C

Simon: Where are you staying?
Alicia: At the Columbia Towers. Do you know it?
Simon: Yes, it's on Granville Street. What's it like?
Alicia: It's excellent.
Simon: Good.

Conversation D

Simon: How do you like the weather here?
Alicia: It's fine. Not too hot. San Diego's pretty hot at this time of year. Anyhow, is it going to rain? I want dry weather for my pictures.
Simon: We get a lot of rain in the fall and winter. December and January are the wettest months. But fortunately the weather forecast is OK for this week.
Alicia: Great.

1 Look at Conversation A. Answer the questions:

  a Which cup is his? Is it the one with a spoon or the one without a spoon?
  b Which cup is hers?
  c Does she take sugar?
  d Does he take sugar?

2 Look at Conversation B. Which of these are good topics for small talk?

  • the city you're in
  • business problems
  • your journey
  • the weather
  • politics
  • food and drink

3 Look at these replies to "What's it like?". Check (✔) the positive answers, and put a cross (✗) next to the negative answers.

Excellent / Not very good / Not too bad / A long way from the center / Very noisy / Busy / Full / Near the airport / Right by the mall / Fine

4 Look at Conversation C, and make a conversation about accommodation.

5 Look at Conversation D, and talk about your town or city. Use these questions:

What's the weather like?
Does it rain in spring / summer / fall / winter?
Which is the hottest / coldest / wettest / driest month?

24 Car Rental Inquiries

Edgar Young wants to rent a car for a few days. He's calling some Car Rental companies.

Clerk: Marathon Rent-a-car. Del Mar office. Can I help you?

Edgar: Yes, I want a full-size sedan for four days. Pick-up in San Diego, drop-off at Los Angeles International Airport. How much will that be?

Clerk: When do you want the car?

Edgar: Today.

Clerk: What time today?

Edgar: Right now. In an hour.

Clerk: I'm sorry. We don't have a full-size available right now.

Edgar: You don't? What do you have?

Clerk: We have just one car available – a specialty convertible. It's a Dodge Viper.

Edgar: A Dodge Viper, eh? Uh … is that expensive?

Clerk: Three hundred dollars.

Edgar: Three hundred a week! Hmm. That's OK.

Clerk: No. Three hundred a day. Plus a fifty-dollar drop-off charge for L.A.

Edgar: You're kidding me.

Clerk: It's a very special car. Sorry. I can call our other offices for you. Or you can call this office later.

Edgar: No, I can call around. Thanks anyway.

MARATHON Car rental groups:

ECONOMY	COMPACT	MID-SIZE	FULL-SIZE	LUXURY	MINIVAN	CONVERTIBLE
Geo Metro	Dodge Shadow	Chevrolet Cavalier	Oldsmobile Cutlass	Lincoln Town Car	Chevrolet Lumina APV	Chrysler le Baron
$140 week $29 daily	$155 week $37 daily	$170 week $47 daily	$230 week $55 daily	$300 week $80 daily	$320 week $84 daily	$300 week $80 daily

Please add: $9 per day for CDW (collision damage waiver).Please add: Personal Accident Protection at $10 per day.

There are drop-off charges for cars returned to our agencies outside the San Diego area.

1 Ask and answer about the car rental information, e.g.

What kind of car is a Chevrolet Cavalier?
How much is a mid-size sedan for a week?
How much is a Lincoln for a day?

2 Role-play the conversation. Use the car rental information, but ask about a different rental group, car make / model, price, etc.

3 👓 Listen to two more phone conversations, and answer the questions.

Call 1 – Alumus Rent-A-Car

a Does he have a pre-reservation?
b Do they have any full-size cars?
c What do they have?
d What's Edgar going to do?

We also have a selection of specialty vehicles including Dodge Vipers, Chevrolet Corvettes, Jaguars, Lexus, and Mercedes (prices on request).

Call 2 – Express Car Rentals

e Do they have full-size vehicles?
f What do they have?
g How much is a luxury car?
h Is that their normal price?
i How much is a mid-size?
j Where does Edgar want to leave the car?
k How much is the drop-off charge?
l What's Edgar going to do?

25 Picking Up a Car

Conversation A

Clerk: Hello. Do you have a pre-reservation?

Edgar: Yes. Young. Edgar Young.

Clerk: OK, Mr. Young, I have it right here. May I see your drivers license?

Edgar: There you go.

Clerk: And this is your current home address?

Edgar: That's right.

Clerk: May I have a contact telephone number?

Edgar: My home number or my hotel in San Diego?

Clerk: Whatever.

Edgar: Home. 604-559-4173.

Clerk: Are there any other drivers?

Edgar: No. Just me.

Clerk: How are you paying for this?

Edgar: Credit card. Visa. There you go.

Clerk: Thank you. What about collision damage waiver and personal accident insurance?

Edgar: Yes, I want both of them.

Clerk: OK. Could you sign your name here … and initial here. Thanks. The car has a full tank of gas. You can return it full, or we can fill it for you.

Conversation B

Edgar: Fine. Do you have a map?

Clerk: Yes, there you go. These are the keys. The car's in the parking lot. It's a white Pontiac Achieve. You can find it in bay 39.

Edgar: Thanks. Uh, does it have air conditioning?

Clerk: Yes. All our cars in California have air conditioning.

Edgar: Good. It's a pretty hot day!

1 Which of these things does Edgar give the clerk?

- ☐ his drivers license
- ☐ some money
- ☐ his credit card
- ☐ a travelers check

Which of these things does the clerk give Edgar?

- ☐ a rental agreement
- ☐ some change
- ☐ a map
- ☐ car keys

2 ★ Communication Activities

Role-play a conversation like Conversation A. You need to complete a form. You can find a form in Section Z. Ask the customer to spell their address.

3 Look at Conversation B. Make a conversation about a different car with this plan:

Bay 34	Bay 35	Bay 36	Bay 37
Cutlass gray	Lumina maroon	Colt white	Lexus beige

Bay 38	Bay 39	Bay 40	Bay 41
Dynasty dark blue	Cavalier gold	Caprice silver	Infiniti bronze

26 Routines

Josie Campbell is with Cecilia Grant on board the _Pacific Rim Voyager_. They're discussing Josie's daily routine.

Cecilia: So, Josie. Let's go through your daily routine. I expect it's the same as on your last ship.

Josie: Sure. When do we begin?

Cecilia: Here. At 7 a.m. First, you always speak to your excursions team.

Josie: OK.

Cecilia: Then passengers usually meet in the Ship's Theater before they leave the ship – that's thirty minutes after we arrive in port.

Josie: And the excursions normally leave thirty minutes later?

Cecilia: That's right. Next, you always check the buses and the passenger list.

Josie: Sure.

Cecilia: Then, after they leave the ship, you generally have time for administration work.

Josie: Do I go on any excursions?

Cecilia: If you have time! You usually don't.

Josie: OK. What about the evenings?

Cecilia: Finally, in the evenings you usually take reservations for the next day.

Josie: It's not exactly the same as my last ship, but it's similar.

Cecilia: Great! Well, the passengers arrive tomorrow morning. You're free this evening.

Josie: Thanks.

Cecilia: Some of us from the entertainment team are going out to dinner. Would you like to come with us? You can meet everyone in an informal setting.

Josie: That's wonderful. Thank you, Cecilia.

1 Ask and answer.

   a What does Josie do first?
   b When do the passengers meet?
   c When do the excursions leave?
   d What does she do next?
   e What does she do then?
   f What does she do in the evenings?
   g Is the routine the same as her last ship?

2 ★ Communication Activities

   Student 1 – use Section C
   Student 2 – use Section O

3 PAIR WORK Ask a partner about their daily routine, e.g.

When do you usually leave home?
What time do you usually arrive at work?
What do you normally do first?
What do you do next?
When do you normally have breaks / lunch?
What time do you normally finish work?
When do you arrive home?

4 Describe your daily routine.

27 Structures

📼 **Simon Chang is explaining his company to Alicia Romero.**
Look at the chart and listen to their conversation.

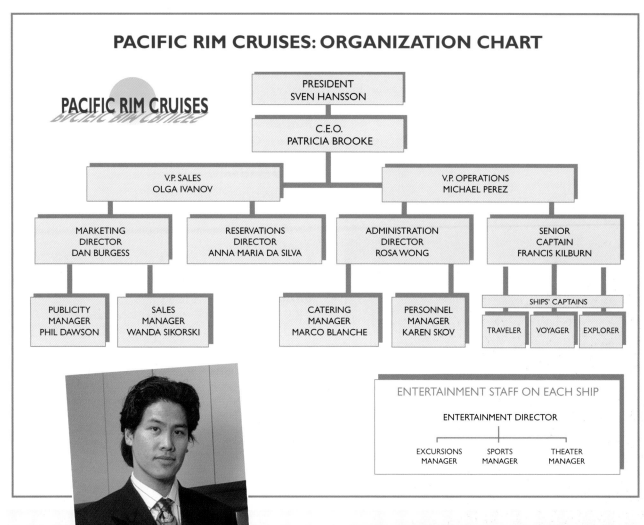

PACIFIC RIM CRUISES: ORGANIZATION CHART

PACIFIC RIM CRUISES

PRESIDENT
SVEN HANSSON

C.E.O.
PATRICIA BROOKE

V.P. SALES
OLGA IVANOV

V.P. OPERATIONS
MICHAEL PEREZ

MARKETING
DIRECTOR
DAN BURGESS

RESERVATIONS
DIRECTOR
ANNA MARIA DA SILVA

ADMINISTRATION
DIRECTOR
ROSA WONG

SENIOR
CAPTAIN
FRANCIS KILBURN

PUBLICITY
MANAGER
PHIL DAWSON

SALES
MANAGER
WANDA SIKORSKI

CATERING
MANAGER
MARCO BLANCHE

PERSONNEL
MANAGER
KAREN SKOV

SHIPS' CAPTAINS

TRAVELER | VOYAGER | EXPLORER

ENTERTAINMENT STAFF ON EACH SHIP

ENTERTAINMENT DIRECTOR

EXCURSIONS
MANAGER | SPORTS
MANAGER | THEATER
MANAGER

1 📼 **Listen again and <u>underline</u> the people Simon talks about.**

2 Find abbreviations on the chart for:

Chief Executive Officer, Vice President

Match these abbreviations with job titles:

Abbreviation	Job title
Mngr.	Head of Department
Dr.	Doctor
Rep.	Manager
H.o.D.	Representative
Asst.	Assistant

3 Ask and answer.

What does Wanda Sikorski do?
She's the Sales Manager.

4 Josie Campbell is the Excursions Manager on board the *Pacific Rim Voyager*. Cecilia Grant is her immediate superior. Can you describe Josie's job in the same way as Simon Chang's job? Look in the Transcripts before you do this.

LANGUAGE BANK		
He's	in charge of	publicity.
She's	responsible for	accounts.
I'm		the Los Angeles office.

He reports to the Sales Director.
They work in the Accounts Department.
Her boss is the Sports Manager.
She has three assistants.
I'm one of her secretaries.
He's my immediate superior.

Conversation A
It's lunchtime in Vancouver.

Simon: OK. It's twelve thirty. You're meeting Mr. Dawson at two. Do you feel like some lunch?

Alicia: Sure.

Simon: What kind of food do you like?

Alicia: Anything. It's up to you.

Simon: I usually go to an Italian place near here. It's self-service, but the food's OK.

Alicia: That's fine. Let's go there.

MENU

TODAY'S ENTREES

Lasagne
Macaroni Cheese
Seafood Pizza
Spaghetti Bolognese

side salad, roll + butter,
beverage $7.98

Conversation B

Simon: Here's a tray. It's a set lunch. They have a choice of four entrees, and you can choose a side salad, a roll and butter, and a drink.

Alicia: Thanks.

Server: Hi. What can I get you?

Alicia: Lasagne, please.

Server: Do you want Parmesan cheese on that?

Alicia: Yes, please.

Simon: Spaghetti Bolognese for me. No Parmesan.

Server: Coming right up.

Conversation C

Cashier: Are those together?

Simon: Yes.

Cashier: That's seventeen dollars and seven cents.

Alicia: Let me pay …

Simon: No. This is on Pacific Rim Cruises.

Alicia: You're sure?

Simon: Of course. I insist.

Alicia: OK. Then let me pay next time …

Cashier: Hey! There's a line at the counter! Make up your minds!

Simon: Sorry. There you go.

DISHES OF THE DAY

Chicken Chow Mein
Sweet & Sour Pork

All served with
boiled rice, tea

$9.00

TODAY'S SPECIALS

Beef Enchiladas
Vegetable tortillas

All with
Guacamole sauce,
refried beans, salad

$8.75

---

1 **Look at Conversation A. Make conversations with this information:**

Student 1: 12:15 p.m. / meeting at 1:45 p.m.
Would you like some lunch?
What sort of food …?
Chinese place downtown

Student 2: 1 p.m. / begin work at 2:15 p.m.
How about some lunch?
What do you feel like?
Mexican restaurant / across the street

2 **Look at Conversation B, and make more conversations using the menus.**

3 **Who's going to pay? Look at Conversation C. Make conversations in groups of three using the Language Bank.**

LANGUAGE BANK
Let me pay.
I'll pay.
This is on me / my company.
No, I'll get it.

29 Dealing With Problems

Conversation A
Pearl Li is working at the front desk at the Columbia Towers Hotel.

Man: Excuse me!
Pearl: Yes, sir?
Man: I want to check out. I'm in a hurry. I have a plane to catch!
Pearl: OK, the cashier's desk is right over there. I'll tell her you're in a hurry.

Conversation B

Pearl: Front desk. This is Pearl speaking.
Phone: I need someone in Room 652 immediately! The shower is running, and it won't stop! There's water all over the floor!
Pearl: Don't worry, sir. I'll send an engineer right away.

Conversation C
Carlos: Housekeeping. Carlos speaking.
Pearl: This is Pearl Li. Carlos, will you go up to room 652 right now? It's urgent.
Carlos: What's the problem?
Pearl: The shower won't stop.
Carlos: I'm on my way.

Conversation D
Pearl: Front desk. This is Pearl …
Phone: This is room 552. Will you send someone quickly? There's water coming through the ceiling!
Pearl: All right. I'll deal with it, ma'am. Front desk. This …
Phone: I'm in room 452, and there's water …

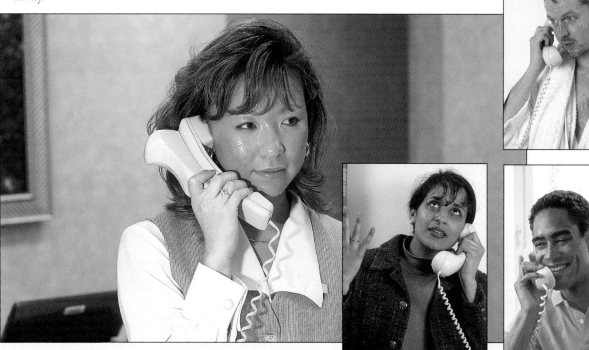

1 **Look through the conversations, and highlight the offers of help.**

2 **There are two requests in the conversations. Highlight them.**

3 **You're a guest at the hotel. You're calling the front desk. Request help in these situations:**

   a The toilet won't work.
   b There are no towels in your room.
   c You want someone to take your bags to the lobby.
   d You're in a hurry. You want the hotel to prepare your bill now, before you come down to the lobby.

**The desk clerk decides who to send.
Use this list:**

room maid / bell captain / engineer / cashier

4 **Imagine that you are the reception clerk. Offer to deal with the problems in activity 3. Then offer help in these situations:**

   • I'm checking out after lunch. I don't want housekeeping to make up my room.
   • I need some stamps.
   • My room's very cold. I can't turn off the air conditioning.
   • The TV isn't working.

30 Arrangements

Conversation A
Jack Hudson is making some phone calls.

Pierre: SaveCash Supermarkets. Pierre speaking.

Jack: Hi, Pierre. This is Jack Hudson. Absolutely Arizona Mineral Waters.

Pierre: Ah, Jack. Yes, how are you?

Jack: I'm fine. I'm in town for a couple of days. Can I come and see you?

Pierre: OK. I'm pretty busy at the moment. Can you make it Friday afternoon?

Jack: Friday afternoon? I'll be there. What time?

Pierre: Anytime after four.

Jack: OK. Does 4:15 suit you?

Pierre: Yes, that's OK. I'll see you then.

Conversation B

Agent: All Canada Airlines. Can I help you?

Jack: Yes. I need a flight from Vancouver to Phoenix on Friday. Do you have any seats?

Agent: Let me see. Yes. I have one on the 5:30 flight.

Jack: Five thirty! What's the check-in time?

Agent: One hour economy. Thirty minutes Business Class. Will you take that?

Jack: No. I won't get to the airport in time. When will the next flight leave?

Agent: There won't be another direct flight on Friday. There'll be one on Saturday at the same time.

Jack: Fine. I'll take it.

Agent: Just let me check. Oh, I'm sorry, that flight's full.

1 Look at Conversation A. Make a conversation with this information:

Alicia Romero / Sagebrush Tours
In town for two weeks.
Is Saturday morning OK? / Not before eleven.
Eleven thirty?

2 Underline 'll, will, and won't in Conversation B. Make a conversation with this information:

Flight to Denver / Saturday lunch / 1:45 flight
No direct flight on Saturday or Sunday
Next flight – Monday at 6:45 a.m.

3 ▣▣ Listen to the agent describing a different route. Find answers to these questions:

a When will the flight leave Vancouver?
b What will the last check-in time be?
c Where will it stop?
d What time will it arrive there?
e When will the next flight leave?
f What time will it arrive in Phoenix?

4 ★ Communication Activities.

Student 1 – use Section D
Student 2 – use Section N

31 Meeting People

Conversation A
Cecilia Grant is introducing Josie to her new *Pacific Rim Voyager* co-workers.

Cecilia: Josie, I want you to meet Kenji Nakamura. He's the Sports Manager. Kenji, this is Josie who's in charge of excursions.
Kenji: How do you do, Josie.
Josie: How do you do.
Kenji: Oh, so you're British.
Josie: That's right.
Kenji: Well, it's good to meet you, Josie.
Josie: And you, Kenji.
Kenji: Everyone calls me Ken.
Josie: OK … Ken.

Conversation B

Cecilia: And this is Britanny Harding. Britanny works in your department. She's a tour guide.
Josie: How do you do, Britanny. I'm Josie Campbell.
Britanny: Pleased to meet you, Josie.
Josie: I'm looking forward to working together.
Britanny: Me, too.

Conversation C
In the ship's control room.

Cecilia: Captain Carlsson? May I introduce Josie Campbell, our new excursions manager?
Carlsson: I'm glad to meet you, Ms. Campbell.

Josie: And I'm glad to meet you, Captain Carlsson.
Carlsson: Aren't you from the *Pacific Rim Traveler*?
Josie: That's right.
Carlsson: Well, I hope you enjoy working with us.
Josie: Thank you, sir.

---

1 Josie meets three people. One has a similar job, one is her superior, and one has a junior job. Answer the questions:

  a Who has a similar job?
  b Who has a junior job?
  c Who is her superior?
  d Does it change the introductions?
  e When do they use first names?

2 <u>Underline</u> the expressions which are about working together in the future.

3 PAIR WORK Write down your name and job title. Exchange it with a partner. Go around the room introducing your partner to other people. Don't forget to shake hands!

LANGUAGE BANK

This is …, and this is …
I want you to meet … / I'd like you to meet …
I want to introduce … / I'd like to introduce …
Can I introduce …? / May I introduce …?

First names, titles

Generally, English speakers use first names very quickly. Some people prefer "diminutives" or friendly forms – Ken, not Kenji. Sue not Susan.

Americans use *sir, madam* more often than the British. Few job titles are used before names, but Captain (military, U.S. police, ships, airplanes) is one of them. Others are Doctor and Professor.

Conversation A

The co-workers from the *Pacific Rim Voyager* are going out for dinner.

Cecilia: Right, we'll need to take a couple of taxis.

Kenji: I don't think so, Cecilia. There are nine of us. We won't get five in one cab.

Cecilia: Yes, you're right. Nine! There's Josie, too. We'll need three cabs then. Ken, you take the first cab with Josie and Britanny.

Kenji: OK … wait! What's the name of the restaurant?

Cecilia: The Panama Hat on Coronado Island. The driver will know it.

Kenji: Where is it exactly? In case he doesn't know.

Cecilia: It's on Orange Avenue.

Conversation B

Cecilia: You'll probably get there first. There's a table for eight, and it's reserved in my name. Ask for an extra chair.

Kenji: No problem.

Cecilia: It's on the company. Get a taxi receipt.

Kenji: Right. See you there.

is also AAA recommended. Tel: 651–3277

PANAMA HAT

3612 Orange Ave, (near corner of Orange and Cabrillo) Coronado Island, 7:30 p.m. – 11:30 p.m.

Excellent restaurant. Good atmosphere. Always reserve tables in advance. Price category: moderate / expensive Tel: 564–9008

1 True or false?

☐ There are five in their party.
☐ There are five passenger seats in U.S. cabs.
☐ They'll need three cabs.
☐ The restaurant isn't well-known.
☐ Orange Avenue is on Coronado Island.

2 Look at Conversation A. Make a conversation with this information:

There are eleven in your party. You're going to take cabs. You want Anna to take the first cab with Michael and Peter. You're going to the Angel of the Desert Restaurant. It's on 7th Avenue and 12th Street.

3 Look at Conversation B. Answer the questions:

a Will Cecilia get there first?
b Ask "Who?"
c Who reserved the table?
d Why will they need an extra chair?

4 ▣▣ Which cabs are they going in? Listen and put the names next to the cabs.

Cecilia / Daniel / The Captain
Laura / Marilyn / Philip
Next cab:
Last cab:

5 ▣▣ Listen to 4 again. Cecilia says "Tell the driver it's the Panama Hat". Are there other instructions she can give Laura? Begin "Tell the driver …"

6 ▣▣ Listen to the cab driver. Ask and answer.

a Does the driver know the restaurant?
b How does he know?

33 About Yourself

Conversation A
Ken and Josie are on their way to the restaurant.

Kenji: OK, Josie. I know you're British, but that's all! Tell me about yourself.

Josie: Mmm, right. Well, I was on the *Pacific Rim Traveler* for two years ... I was a tour guide. And ... uh, I live in Vancouver, and, uh... what do you want to know?

Kenji: What were you before you were a tour guide?

Josie: Before? I was a reservations clerk with Cunard in Europe, and before that I was a student. I was in college for three years. I have a degree in tourism.

Conversation B

Josie: Come on! It's your turn!

Kenji: Me? I was a pro tennis player before this job.

Josie: You were a professional?

Kenji: Oh, yeah. I was good, pretty good. But I wasn't fantastic. Then I was a sports coach last year, and this year I'm the Sports Manager.

Josie: Were you in matches with any of the stars?

Kenji: Some. I was in a lot of tournaments. I live in San Diego. It's my home town. I was born here.

1 Look at Conversation A. Ask and answer.

 a Where was Josie born?
 b How long was Josie on the *Pacific Rim Traveler*?
 c What was her job?
 d What was she before that?
 e Where was she a reservations clerk?
 f How long was she in college?
 g Does she have any qualifications?

2 Look at Conversation B. Ask and answer.

 a Where was Ken born?
 b What was he before he was a sports coach?
 c Was he an amateur or was he a professional?
 d Was he good? Was he fantastic?
 e What was his job last year?
 f Was he in matches with any famous tennis players?

3 ★ Communication Activities

Student 1 – use Section E
Student 2 – use Section Y

4 PAIR WORK Interview a partner. Ask these questions:

Where were you born?
Where were you at school / college?
Do you have any qualifications?
What was your first job?
How long were you in that job?
What was your next / last job?

5 PAIR WORK Change partners. Ask your new partner about their first partner, e.g.

Where was (she) at school?
What was (his) first job?

34 Getting Through

How easy is it to get through to people in companies?

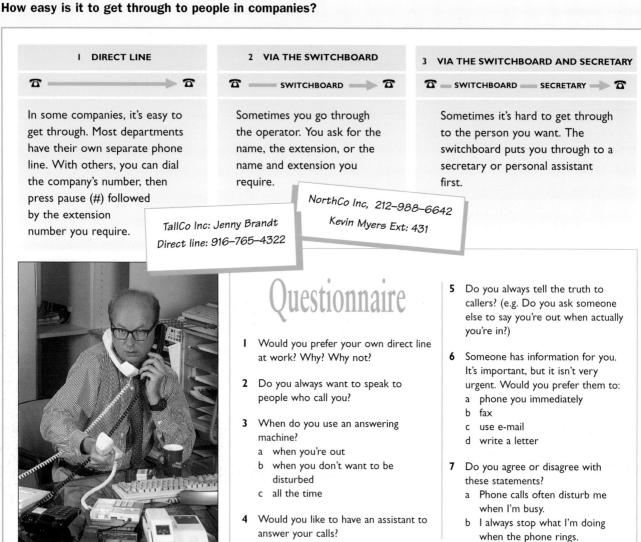

1 DIRECT LINE	2 VIA THE SWITCHBOARD	3 VIA THE SWITCHBOARD AND SECRETARY
☎ ➝ ☎	☎ ➝ SWITCHBOARD ➝ ☎	☎ ➝ SWITCHBOARD ➝ SECRETARY ➝ ☎
In some companies, it's easy to get through. Most departments have their own separate phone line. With others, you can dial the company's number, then press pause (#) followed by the extension number you require.	Sometimes you go through the operator. You ask for the name, the extension, or the name and extension you require.	Sometimes it's hard to get through to the person you want. The switchboard puts you through to a secretary or personal assistant first.

TallCo Inc: Jenny Brandt
Direct line: 916–765–4322

NorthCo Inc, 212–988–6642
Kevin Myers Ext: 431

Questionnaire

1 Would you prefer your own direct line at work? Why? Why not?

2 Do you always want to speak to people who call you?

3 When do you use an answering machine?
 a when you're out
 b when you don't want to be disturbed
 c all the time

4 Would you like to have an assistant to answer your calls?

5 Do you always tell the truth to callers? (e.g. Do you ask someone else to say you're out when actually you're in?)

6 Someone has information for you. It's important, but it isn't very urgent. Would you prefer them to:
 a phone you immediately
 b fax
 c use e-mail
 d write a letter

7 Do you agree or disagree with these statements?
 a Phone calls often disturb me when I'm busy.
 b I always stop what I'm doing when the phone rings.

---

1 PAIR WORK Interview a partner and complete the questionnaire.

2 📼 Part 1. Edgar is calling Simon. Listen to Edgar's phone call, and complete the blanks:

Edgar: I want ____ speak ____ Simon Chang, ____ .

Operator: ____ may I ____ who's calling?
Edgar: Yes. ____ is Edgar Young ____ AmCan Travel.
Operator: Thank you, Mr. Young. Please ____ .

3 📼 Part 2. Answer the questions:

a What's Simon doing?
b Does he want to speak with Edgar?
c What are Simon's instructions to the secretary?
d What does the secretary ask the operator to do?

4 📼 Part 3. Complete the blanks:

I'm ____ he's in a meeting. Can I take a ____ ?
Can't you ____ him?
I'm ____ not.
Do you want ____ to call ____ back?
I guess ____ .

Ask and answer.

a Who says the above lines?
b Where is Edgar?
c Does Simon know this?

5 PAIR WORK Write three things you want to do in the next week. Ask about your partner's list. Write three things you want other people to do for you. Ask about your partner's list.

35 Explaining

Conversation A
Simon is with Alicia in his office at Pacific Rim Cruises. He puts the phone down.
Simon: Phew! That was Edgar Young on the line.
Alicia: Sorry?
Simon: Edgar, AmCan? Don't you know him?
Alicia: No.
Simon: I'm surprised, because AmCan is the biggest travel agency in North America.
Alicia: Oh, yes. Their ads were on TV last night.

Conversation B
Alicia: So who's Edgar Young?
Simon: He's the boss of AmCan's Vancouver office.
Alicia: So he's Canadian.
Simon: No, he's American. From Florida.
Alicia: And so you don't want to speak with him because I'm here?
Simon: I don't want to speak with him period!

North American Brochure

1 🔊 **Listen to Simon and Alicia. Are these statements true or false? What do you think?**

☐ AmCan represents both cruise lines.
☐ Albion-America has more ships than Pacific Rim.
☐ Albion-America is part of the AmCan Travel Corporation.
☐ Pacific Rim doesn't pay large commissions.
☐ Albion-America does pay large commissions.

2 Ask and answer.

a Alicia doesn't know Edgar. Why is Simon surprised?
b Why does Edgar want to talk with Simon?
c Why doesn't Pacific Rim want to do business with AmCan Travel?

PACIFIC RIM CRUISES
INTERNAL MEMO

From: Simon Chang, Publicity Dept.
To: Mr. P. Dawson, Publicity Manager
Subject: AmCan Travel

AmCan Travel is the biggest Travel Agency in North America, __ they have thirty regional offices. They represent Albion-America __ advertise them in all their brochures. They want a meeting __ they want to represent Pacific Rim, __ I don't think a deal is a good idea. There are two reasons for my opinion. First, __ they will ask for a large commission. Second, __ we don't want to be advertised on the same pages with Albion-American.

3 This is Simon's report on AmCan travel. Complete the blanks with *and*, *but*, or *because*.

36 Punctuation

Look at this letter. The punctuation is missing.

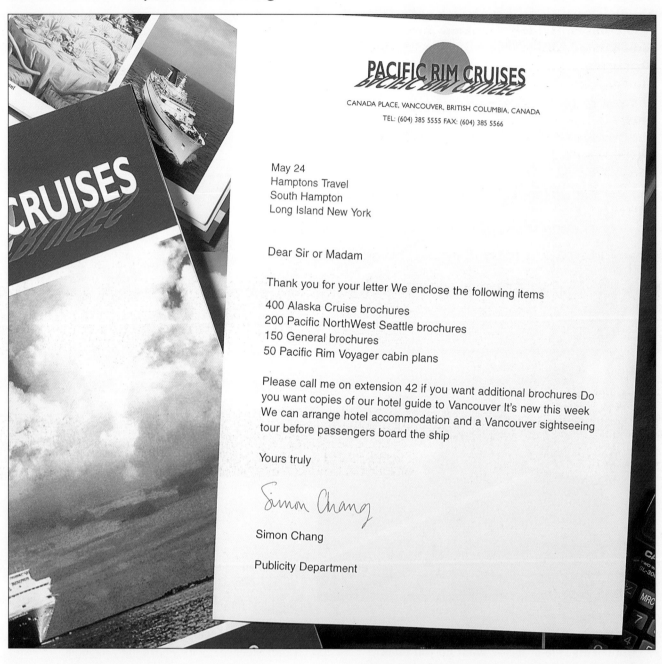

PACIFIC RIM CRUISES

CANADA PLACE, VANCOUVER, BRITISH COLUMBIA, CANADA
TEL: (604) 385 5555 FAX: (604) 385 5566

May 24
Hamptons Travel
South Hampton
Long Island New York

Dear Sir or Madam

Thank you for your letter We enclose the following items

400 Alaska Cruise brochures
200 Pacific NorthWest Seattle brochures
150 General brochures
50 Pacific Rim Voyager cabin plans

Please call me on extension 42 if you want additional brochures Do you want copies of our hotel guide to Vancouver It's new this week We can arrange hotel accommodation and a Vancouver sightseeing tour before passengers board the ship

Yours truly

Simon Chang

Simon Chang

Publicity Department

---

1 Put the punctuation marks in the boxes:

> Punctuation marks: ? – ! , " " . : / ( )

- [ ] parentheses (U.K. brackets)
- [ ] period (U.K. full stop)
- [ ] quotation marks
- [ ] exclamation point
- [ ] question mark
- [ ] slash
- [ ] colon
- [ ] comma
- [ ] dash

2 🔊 Part 1. The letter above has no punctuation. Listen to Simon dictating the letter. Listen to his pauses and intonation. What do you think the punctuation marks are?

3 🔊 Part 2. Listen again. This time Simon is dictating the punctuation. Write in the marks.

4 ★ Communication Activities

Student 1 – use Section F
Student 2 – use Section L

37 Polite Inquiries

Conversation A

Simon Chang's boss, Mr. Dawson, is meeting Alicia Romero for the first time. They are in Mr. Dawson's office at Pacific Rim Cruises in Vancouver.

Mr. Dawson: Ah, you must be Ms. Romero. How do you do. I'm Phil Dawson.

Alicia: Glad to meet you. Please call me Alicia.

Mr. Dawson: Thanks, Alicia. Call me Phil. Did you have a good flight?

Alicia: Yes, I did. It was fine.

Mr. Dawson: Was the plane on time?

Alicia: Yes, it was right on time.

Conversation B

Mr. Dawson: I'm sorry I wasn't here this morning. I was on one of our ships. Did you have lunch?

Alicia: Yes, I had lunch with Simon.

Mr. Dawson: Where did you go?

Alicia: We went to an Italian place near the office.

Mr. Dawson: Yes, I know it. Was everything OK?

Alicia: Yes, thanks. It was very good.

Mr: Dawson: Did you have their pizza? They do great pizza.

Alicia: No, I didn't. I had the lasagne. It was OK.

Mr. Dawson: Try the pizza next time! Well, Simon's going to look after you during your visit. If you have any questions, you can ask me anytime.

1 Mr. Dawson asks several questions. He doesn't ask because he needs information. He's trying to be polite and friendly. <u>Underline</u> his questions.

2 Ask and answer.

  a Did Alicia have a good flight?
  b Was it on time?
  c Did she have lunch with Mr. Dawson?
  d Who did she have lunch with?
  e Did she have pizza?
  f What did she have?

3 Look at Conversations A and B, and <u>underline</u> all the sentences which contain a past tense.

4 PAIR WORK **Ask a partner these questions:**

  What did you have for breakfast?
  When did you have lunch?
  Where did you go for lunch?
  What did you have for lunch?
  Did you go out last weekend?
  Where did you go?
  Did you have a vacation last year?
  Where did you go?

38 Laundry

Conversation A
Morning: Edgar Young is at his hotel.

Edgar: Morning. I have some laundry in room 213.
Valet: 213? Did you put a laundry list in the bag?
Edgar: Yes, I did.
Valet: OK. Somebody will be right up. Leave the bag behind the door.

Conversation B
Evening: Edgar's back in his room.

Rita: Housekeeping. Rita speaking.
Edgar: Ah, right. Where's my laundry?
Rita: Sorry, who is this?
Edgar: My name's Young, room 213.
Rita: And you have a problem with your laundry?
Edgar: Yes, I do! I left it in my room for same day service. And it isn't back.

Rita: Did you tell the valet that it was in your room?
Edgar: Yes, I did.
Rita: When did you call them?
Edgar: I called them at eight fifteen.
Rita: You were too late. The last time for same day service is eight o'clock, Mr. Young. I'm sorry, but you'll get it tomorrow.

Quantity Inn
San Diego
LAUNDRY LIST

DATE: ....
NAME: ....
....
ROOM NO: ....

Check service required:
- ☐ Regular (next day 7 p.m.)
- ☐ Same day service (Pick up by 8 a.m., return by 7 p.m.)
- ☐ Overnight (add 50%)

MENS		no of items	WOMENS		no of items
Shirts	$4.00		Blouse	$4.00	
T-shirts	$3.00		Dress (wash)	$5.00	
Undershorts	$2.00		Skirt	$4.00	
Pants (wash)	$4.50		Nightgown	$3.50	
Pajamas	$4.50		Slacks (wash)	$4.50	
Shorts	$3.00		Underwear	$2.00	
Sweatshirts	$4.00		Pantyhose	$1.50	
Socks (pair)	$1.50		Robe	$4.50	
TOTALS			TOTALS		

Special instructions:

If the list is not completed our count must be accepted. In case of loss or damage, liability is limited to ten times the price charged. We are not responsible for shrinkage, color fastness, zippers, or articles left in clothing.

Guest signature:

1 Ask and answer.
  a When did Edgar call the valet service?
  b Was this too early or too late?
  c What's the last time for same-day service?
  d Did he put a list in the bag?
  e Where did he leave the bag?

2 Look at the laundry list. Check (✔) the items of clothing you wear BELOW the waist. <u>Underline items you wear ABOVE the waist.</u> Circle items you wear above AND below the waist.

3 The fifteen items you sent to the laundry this morning aren't back. You didn't put your name and room number on the bag. You're calling housekeeping. They ask: "What was in the bag?" Tell them, e.g.

There were three shirts.

4 Make a list of the things you took on your last vacation or business trip. Compare your list with a partner, e.g.

How many (pairs of shoes) did you take?
Did you take too many shoes?
Did you wear everything / forget anything?

38

39 Important Messages

Conversation A

Jack is at the Pioneer Hotel in Vancouver.

Jack: The key to room 47, please.

Clerk: There you go. Uh, wait up, there are a couple of messages for you.

Jack: OK. What are they?

Clerk: Here's a fax. It came about an hour ago.

Jack: 'Call Pierre, SaveCash Supermarkets, at home.'

Clerk: And here's the other one. It's a phone message. I wrote it down.

Jack: 'Call me Wednesday night, Samuel Davies.' But it's Thursday today.

Clerk: Yes, I didn't give it to you yesterday. Sorry.

Jack: Anyhow, I don't know any Samuel Davies.

Clerk: Huh! Maybe it was David Samuels? Or maybe the message was for someone else.

Jack: Well, it's too late now. Did Pierre leave a telephone number?

Clerk: No, he didn't.

Conversation B

Jack: Pierre's home number … I wrote it down on a piece of paper somewhere … Now, where did I put it? It's somewhere in here …

Housekeeping: Yes, sir?

Jack: There was a piece of paper on my bedside table this morning. It isn't here now.

Housekeeping: I'm sorry. Was it important?

Jack: Of course it was! There were some telephone numbers on the paper.

Housekeeping: I can ask your room maid. What was the paper like?

Jack: It was a scrap of paper, small, mm, half a page.

Housekeeping: Just a scrap of paper? Did you look in the trash?

Jack: Yes, I did. It's empty.

Housekeeping: I'm sorry.

1 Look at Conversation A. Answer the questions:

   a When did the fax come?

   b When did the phone message come?

   c Was the message clear?

Look at Conversation B. Answer the questions:

   d Where did Jack write the number down?

   e Where did he leave it?

   f Is it there now?

   g Describe the paper.

   h Did he look in the trash?

   i Was it in there?

   j What's he going to do next?

2 Listen to these three phone messages. Note the messages down.

3 Which of the expressions in the language bank do you hear in the listening?

LANGUAGE BANK
Can you repeat that?
Can you say that again?
Can you spell that?
Let me check that.
Let me read that back to you.
Does (he) have your number?

4 Write down three short messages. Role-play a phone conversation. Your partner writes them down.

40 Telephone Services

1 **Complete the table with the numbers from your country:**

	Emergency Services	Directory Assistance	International Access Code	International Directory
U.S.A. / Canada	911	1 + area code + 555 - 1212	011+ country code	00
U.K.	999	192	00 + country code	153
My country				

Calling another country from the U.S.A. and Canada:

e.g. You want to call British Computers plc. The number on their stationary is 0171-353-2841.

The first "0" is the access code from inside the U.K. Delete it.

You press:

International Access Code	+	Country Code	+	Area Code	+	Number
011		(U.K.) 44		(London) 171		353–2841

Country codes:

Here are some country codes:

Australia	61	France	33	Japan	81
Argentina	54	Germany	49	Korea	82
Brazil	55	Greece	30	Mexico	52
China	86	Ireland	353	Thailand	66
Columbia	57	Italy	39	U.K.	44

Area codes:

Here are some area codes:

Kyoto	75	Seoul	2	Buenos Aries	1
Paris	1	Berlin	30	Melbourne	3
Athens	1	Beijing	1	Rio de Janeiro	21
Donegal	73	Bangkok	2	Acapulco	748
Cartagena	53	Bologna	51	Nottingham	115

2 **Write down five imaginary telephone numbers in the cities under area codes. Ask your partner to tell you how to call them:**

- from the U.S.A. or Canada
- from your country

3 👓 **Listen to Jack Hudson finding two numbers from directory assistance. Write the numbers down:**

First number: _____
Second number: _____

4 **Which of these services can you get from telephones in your country?**

- directory assistance
- a time check
- a weather forecast
- sports results
- traffic information
- toll free numbers

5 **Compare with your country. Ask and answer.**

- Do the above services have a recorded message or an operator?
- Is directory assistance free?
- Are there more pay phones, phone card phones, or credit card phones? Which do you prefer? Why?

Alicia and Simon are planning next week's schedule. Alicia is going to take pictures of tourist attractions in the Vancouver area for the brochure.

Grouse Mountain

Gastown

Capilano Suspension Bridge

TO: Ms. A. Romero

Photo Shoot: Provisional schedule

Monday 28:
Downtown – Canada Place, Columbia Towers (exterior and interior)

Tuesday 29:
a.m. Downtown – Gastown, Chinatown
p.m. Stanley Park

Wednesday 30:
All day – Float plane flightseeing ride

Thursday 31:
Seabus to North Vancouver + harbor views
Capilano Suspension Bridge, Grouse Mountain

Friday 1:
Extra day – in case of bad weather on other days

Saturday 2:
FREE

Sunday 3:
9.00 Canada Place – ship arrives at 10 a.m.

Seabus to North Vancouver

1 Ask and answer about the schedule, e.g.

When are they going to be in Chinatown?
What are they going to do on Thursday?

2 📼 **Listen to Simon describing some of the attractions. Number the photographs above.**

3 Read the Transcripts of his descriptions. <u>Underline</u> the things Alicia can photograph.

4 Describe three attractions in your area using the Language Bank.

LANGUAGE BANK
This is a bridge / mountain / river / area of the city / park / historic building / square.
There are great views. You can see ... / ride ... / go on ...
It's good for children / adults / older people.
It's famous / popular because ... I like it because ...
I often / sometimes / occasionally go there.

41

42 Suggestions

Conversation A

Jack Hudson is calling Pierre Duchamps.

Pierre: Hello? Pierre Duchamps.

Jack: Hello, Pierre. This is Jack Hudson. I'm returning your call.

Pierre: Ah, Jack. How are you?

Jack: Sorry to disturb you at home.

Pierre: That's all right.

Jack: I'm not interrupting your meal, am I?

Pierre: Uh … no. No, not at all.

Conversation B

Pierre: Thanks for calling back. I had an idea.

Jack: Yes?

Pierre: This is just a suggestion. Why don't you call Pacific Rim Cruises?

Jack: Pacific Rim. Why?

Pierre: They have a big catering department. You should tell them about Absolutely Arizona Mineral water.

Jack: You think so?

Pierre: Yes, you should. Why don't you try them tomorrow?

Jack: Why not? OK, I will. Thanks for the idea.

Pierre: You're welcome. I'll see you tomorrow.

1 **Look at Conversation A, and make more conversations using the Language Bank.**

LANGUAGE BANK	
Apologizing for disturbing someone	Returning a call
Sorry to disturb you (at home / lunch)	I'm returning your call.
Am I interrupting anything?	I'm calling you back.
I'm not interrupting (you), am I?	I had a message to call you.
Are you busy right now?	You tried to call me earlier.

2 **Your partner wants to buy a present for someone. Give advice from the Language Bank, e.g.**

　　A: I want a gift for my (son).　**B:** How old is (he)?

A: (He)'s six.　**B:** Why don't you get (him) a bike.
A: That's a good idea.

LANGUAGE BANK	
Suggestions / advice	Replies
Why don't you (call them)?	(✔) OK. That's a good idea. I will.
You should (call them).	I don't know …
I suggest (you call them).	(✘) I'm not sure about that.
What about calling them?	I don't think I will.

You can use this vocabulary:

nephew (12) niece (8) uncle (50) aunt (45)
brother (23) sister (18) wife (35) boyfriend (20)

3 **Your partner wants to be fitter and healthier. Give strong suggestions and advice, e.g.**

You should drink more water / play a sport.

43 The Menu

The party from the *Pacific Rim Voyager* are in the Panama Hat restaurant.

The Panama Hat.

Orange Avenue, Coronado Island, San Diego, Ca.

MENU

Starters

New England clam chowder	$4.50
Spinach and bacon salad	$3.95
Melon with genuine Italian Parma ham	$4.25
Italian tomato and mozzarella cheese salad with basil	$5.45

Entrées

Grilled tuna steak with fresh lemon sauce ...	$15.95
Seafood selection – deep fried fish, shrimp ..	$14.50
Charcoal grilled 16 oz beefsteak, Texas barbecue sauce	$17.00
Chef's salad (turkey, ham, egg, Swiss cheese)	$12.95
Stir-fried market vegetables with .... Japanese noodles (vegetarian)	$11.75

All entrées served with a choice of salad, baked Idaho potato or French fries, vegetable selection, and bread roll

Desserts

Florida Key lime pie.	$5.95
California strawberries	$3.00
Mom's apple pie, with Oregon apples	$3.25

Beverages

Ask for our extensive wine list – we have more than 100 wines by the bottle

Mineral water .... *Arrowhead, Clearly Canadian, San Pellegrino*	$1.50
House white .... *California Chardonnay*	$6.75 a glass
House red .... *California Zinfandel*	$6.75 a glass
House rosé .... *California Blush*	$6.75 a glass

---

1 Read through the menu.

a List the names of countries and American states that you see.

b How many methods of cooking are there on the menu? List them.

2 Read through the menu again. Make three lists:

Meat dishes; Fish dishes; Vegetarian dishes

3 ◉◉ **Listen to the waiter. He's describing one of the dishes. Ask and answer.**

Which of these foods does the waiter mention?
tuna ☐	olive oil ☐	spinach ☐	lettuce ☐
basil ☐	ketchup ☐	pepper ☐	lemons ☐
salt ☐	eggplant ☐	shrimp ☐	tomato ☐
garlic ☐	potatoes ☐	zucchini ☐	onion ☐

What color are the foods on the list? e.g. Spinach is dark green.

Do waiters talk this much in your country? Do they tell you their names?

4 ◉◉ **Listen to three people giving their orders. Note what they order and the words they use for requests.**

Cecilia: _____

Ken: _____

Josie: _____

5 PAIR WORK Role-play a waiter and a customer. Order a meal from the menu.

44 At the Table

Conversation A
The party from the ship is waiting for their first course at the Panama Hat restaurant.

Cecilia: Can you pass me the bread, Josie?
Josie: There you go. And the butter?
Cecilia: No, thanks.
Josie: Ken?
Kenji: Yes, please. Mm. It's warm. That's good. Aren't you having any bread, Josie?
Josie: Not for me, thanks.

Conversation B
Waiter: Hi … Who ordered the melon?
Cecilia: That's for me.
Waiter: And whose is the tomato and mozzarella?
Josie: That's mine. Thank you very much.
Waiter: You're welcome. And the clam chowder? Did anybody order the clam chowder?
Kenji: It's not mine.
Waiter: Pardon me … whose is the clam chowder? I'm sorry. What did you order, sir?
Kenji: I ordered the spinach and bacon salad, not the chowder.
Waiter: Hmm. There must be a mistake. I'm really sorry. I'll be right back with your salad.

Conversation C
Kenji: Hey, don't wait for me. Please start.
Josie: Thanks. Do you want to try some of my salad?
Kenji: It looks really good … are you sure?
Josie: Sure I'm sure. Go ahead … help yourself.
Kenji: Great. Well, enjoy your meal!

1 Look at Conversation A, and make more conversations using the Language Bank.

LANGUAGE BANK	
Could **you** pass (**me**) the bread?	Sure
Can **you** pass (**him**) the bread?	There you go
May **I** have the bread?	Here it is

bread / butter / salt / pepper / water / ice

2 Look at Conversation B and the menu entrées from Unit 43. Make a conversation with a waiter who has these items for five of you at a table:

two of the same items for John and Anna
one item for Peter
one item for Diana
one item for you

3 Look at Conversation C. Complete the blanks.

a Don't worry. I can help ____ .
b Anna, please help ____ to salad.
c Come on everybody! You can all help ____ .
d Tell Maria to help ____ to wine.
e Good. We can all help ____ to soup.
f Ask him to help ____ to vegetables.

4 PAIR WORK Ask a partner about restaurants.

Do you offer to pass people food?
Do you ask people to pass you food?
Do you offer people food from your plate?
Do you take food from other people's plates?
Do you talk about business during the meal?
When do you talk about business in a restaurant?
Do you have a special word for toasts?
Do you invite people to enjoy their meal? What do you say?

Ken and Josie are talking during the meal at the Panama Hat in San Diego.

Josie: Tell me, Ken, what do you like doing in your free time?

Kenji: What free time? We don't have much free time in this job!

Josie: Oh, come on! I mean, do you like playing tennis?

Kenji: Well, yes. It's my job, but I enjoy playing tennis outside work, too. What about you?

Josie: I like doing aerobics, and I like dancing, and I love swimming!

Kenji: And tennis?

Josie: I like playing, but I'm not very good at tennis. I love watching it, though.

Kenji: I can give you some lessons, if you like.

Josie: Really? That's very kind of you.

Kenji: No problem.

playing tennis playing golf playing baseball	doing yoga doing aerobics weight-training
swimming jogging (go) dancing	hiking camping sailing
doing crosswords collecting things playing computer games	going to movies going to the theater eating out
reading drawing painting	listening to music watching sport watching TV

1 **Which of these things do you like doing? Check (✔) them.**
Which of these things do you really dislike doing? Put a cross (✗).

2 **Match these titles to the eight boxes.**
out in the country / going out for entertainment / artistic activities / the beautiful body / competitive sport / passive activities / getting fit / intellectual activities

3 PAIR WORK **Ask a partner about the boxes, e.g.**
How many checks do you have?
How many crosses do you have?
Do you like (jogging)?
How often do you (jog)?
Are you good at (swimming)?

4 PAIR WORK **Change partners and ask about their previous partner, e.g.**
Does she like (doing crosswords)?
How often does she (do crosswords)?
Is he good at (swimming)?

5 **Look at your partner's checks and crosses. Ask and answer.**
Are they an indoor person or an outdoor person?
Do they like doing things alone or with others?
Do they like competition when they do exercise?
Do they like active things (doing things) or passive things (watching things)?

46 E-Mail

Read e-mail etiquette and the message which Pacific Rim Cruises sent to Cruise Supply Co.

E-MAIL ETIQUETTE

- Typing in capitals is like SHOUTING. Don't do it.
- Be careful about the e-mail address. You don't want other people to see your message.
- Keep messages short, simple, and clear. Short messages get more replies!
- Never send rude messages by e-mail.
- If you're downloading a large file, send a short message first.
- Color photos of your face or funny pictures use a lot of time and computer memory. The other person doesn't want to wait five minutes to see your picture.

1 Stefan has a business message and a personal message. Ask and answer.

a Which is he receiving?
b Which is he sending?
c Who is the message from?
d What's the date and time of the message?
e Does Pacific Rim normally buy goods from the Cruise Supply Company?
f Is this an extra order, or is it the main order?
g Who's Stefan meeting for lunch? When?

2 People often leave out words in e-mail. What words are missing from these lines?

Please deliver Sunday June 3
Pacific Rim Voyager – invoice us
Please call Sunday
Deliver items Tuesday
Will meet August
See you restaurant 6 p.m.

3 Match the abbreviations to their meanings. The symbols are a "happy face" on its side.

FAO   I'm kidding / joking
:-(I regret (= I'm sorry)
TIA   for the attention of
re   reference (with reference to)
RGT   I'm unhappy about (this)
INFO   estimated time of arrival
ETA   thanks in advance
:-)   information

4 PAIR WORK Interview a partner, and complete the questionnaire.

E-MAIL QUESTIONNAIRE

1 Which methods can you use to order goods?
☐ letter ☐ fax ☐ phone ☐ e-mail

2 If you use phone, fax, or e-mail, do you also send a letter? Why?

3 Which of these things do you need to send e-mail?
☐ a computer ☐ a fax machine
☐ a phone line ☐ a telephone
☐ a photocopier ☐ a modem

4 How can you use e-mail?
☐ on a network inside your company
☐ for messages to friends
☐ to speak to strangers on the Internet
☐ to contact other companies

5 Do you use e-mail? How often?

6 Are you / your company on the Internet?

47 Sales Talk

Conversation A

Jack Hudson is at the offices of Pacific Rim Cruises. It's Friday May 26th.

Marsha: Hold on, there's someone at the door. Come in!

Jack: Good morning. Ms. Irving?

Marsha: Yes, I'm Marsha Irving. Uh, do you have an appointment?

Jack: Jack Hudson? Absolutely Arizona Mineral Waters? This is my card.

Marsha: Oh, yes. You're very early ... excuse me ... Stefan, can I call you back? I have a visitor. OK. In about twenty minutes.

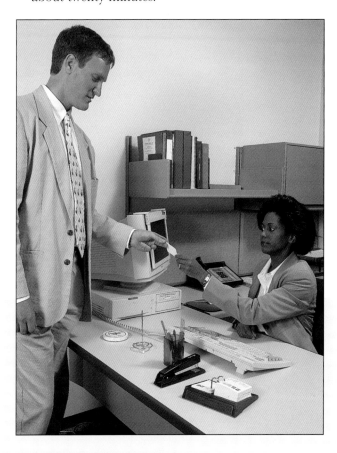

Conversation B

Jack: I just want you to try this.

Marsha: Pardon me?

Jack: I want you to try a glass of Absolutely Arizona ... before I say anything.

Marsha: OK. Mm. Yes, it's all right.

Jack: All right? This is the best mineral water in North America. It's produced and bottled in Arizona, and ...

Marsha: Did you say 'Arizona'?

Jack: Yes, ma'am. I did.

Marsha: But Arizona's one of the driest states ... it's desert, isn't it?

Jack: It's not all desert. This comes from high in the mountains.

Marsha: But our passengers want well-known brand names. Perrier, Evian.

Jack: I can give you a very special deal ... we have a lot of Absolutely Arizona here in Vancouver. We can deliver immediately. You can try it out on your next cruise.

Marsha: I'm sorry, Mr. Hudson. You're wasting your time. You see, I just placed an order for our next cruise. Sorry.

Then list some well-known brand names.

What do they make?
Where are they made?

3 PAIR WORK **Ask and answer.**

Which is the ...
a ... biggest country in North America?
b ... biggest city in the U.S.A.?
c ... best cola drink in your opinion?
d ... the coldest state in the U.S.A.?
e ... the hottest state in the U.S.A.?
f ... the wettest state in the U.S.A.?

4 📟 **Listen to Marsha's phone call. Role-play Marsha's conversation with Jack Hudson. What is she going to say?**

5 ★ **Communication Activities**

Student 1 – use Section G
Student 2 – use Section Q

1 Find the expressions where ...

- Jack tries to sell the mineral water.
- Marsha says she isn't interested.

2 Ask and answer about these products, e.g.

Where is Evian produced?
It's produced and bottled in France.
Perrier / San Pelligrino / Clearly Canadian

Where are Cadillac cars made?
Toyota / Renault / Fiat / Jaguar

Where is oil produced?
wine / Hershey's chocolate / beer

48 Flightseeing

It's Wednesday May 30th. Alicia is talking to Simon about her flightseeing trip.

"I took some great pictures! It was a fantastic trip. There were only four of us, and we went on a small floatplane. We took off from Vancouver Harbour and flew for about forty minutes. We flew right over the mountains, and then we landed on a small lake high up in the mountains. You can't get there on foot. Well, you can, but it's a two-day hike and climb. You can only get there easily by floatplane. The plane taxied across the lake, and we got down onto a small beach. Our pilot had a picnic lunch in the plane, and he gave us sandwiches and drinks. It was so quiet, and the air was so clean! The pilot had a spray can of bear deterrent because there are bears in the mountains, but we didn't see any. We stayed there for about an hour. We took off and circled around the lake three times … we weren't high enough to get over the mountain the first time. Finally, we made it over the mountain and flew back here … and landed on the harbor. We have to put these pictures in our brochure!"

1 Find the past of these verbs:

take off / fly / have / stay / take / go / land / get / walk / make / circle / give / taxi

Which are regular? Which are irregular? Which can you use to talk about airplanes?

2 Ask and answer.

a Where did they take off from / land?
b How long was the flight?
c How did the plane get to the beach?
d What did the pilot give them?
e How many bears did they see?
f How long did they stay there?
g Was the take-off easy?
h What did they do?

3 PAIR WORK Ask a partner about their last vacation using the Language Bank.

Where were you?   Who was with you?
What did you do?   Where did you go?
How did you travel?   What did you see?

LANGUAGE BANK			
mountain	hill	museum	valley
theater	river	bridge	lake
park	island	harbor	desert
building	ocean	beach	forest

49 Let's Make a Deal

Conversation A
It's Thursday May 31st. Edgar Young is meeting Cathy Lowe at Sagebrush Tours.

Edgar: Thank you for seeing me, Ms. Lowe.

Cathy: Yes. I'm sorry I couldn't meet with you last week. I was out of town for a few days. I hope it wasn't inconvenient.

Edgar: No, I decided to stay in San Diego a few more days anyway.

Conversation B

Cathy: Well, what can I do for you?

Edgar: It's about your brochure for next year. You have Pacific Rim Cruises in your brochure.

Cathy: That's right.

Edgar: AmCan Travel represents Albion-America, and we have Alaska cruises also. In fact, we have more ships, and we carry more passengers. We're cheaper and bigger. We also offer a greater commission to travel agents.

Cathy: Yes, I know Albion-America.

Edgar: Look, let's make a deal. We can offer five per cent more than Pacific Rim, and …

Cathy: But we're very happy with Pacific Rim. I'm sorry, but we're not interested.

Conversation C

Edgar: There's something else, too. We like your brochure very much indeed.

Cathy: Thank you.

Edgar: You have a great photographer.

Cathy: Alicia Romero? She's the best.

Edgar: Yes. Alicia Romero. We'd like her to do our new brochure. Can I meet her?

Cathy: I'm sorry, Mr. Young. Alicia's in Vancouver right now. She's taking photographs for us … and for Pacific Rim Cruises.

Edgar: What? I don't believe it! You mean, she's in Vancouver and I'm down here?

Cathy: That's right. Sorry.

1 Look at Conversation A. Cathy didn't meet him last week because she was out of town for a few days. What does she say?
Apologize in these situations:

You didn't finish the work. You had a dental appointment.
You didn't get to the meeting on time. You couldn't find a parking space.

2 ★ Communication Activities

Student 1 – use the table
Student 2 – use Section S

3 Compare Albion-America and Pacific Rim Cruises, e.g.

Albion-America has more ships.
Pacific Rim Cruises has fewer ships.

	Albion-America	Pacific Rim Cruises
number of ships		3
average age of ships		5 years
average number of cabins per ship		275
passengers last year		62,500
cabins with balconies		240 on each ship
restaurants per ship		three
cinemas per ship		one
video channels on TV		eight
swimming pools per ship		one
average vacation cost for 7 days		$3,450

50 Gas Station

Conversation A
Edgar Young is returning his rental car at LAX (Los Angeles International Airport).

Edgar: Are there many more questions? I have a flight to catch.

Clerk: I understand that, sir. Does the car have a full tank of gas?

Edgar: No, I was in a hurry. You can fill it.

Clerk: Yes, we can. But there's a $3 charge per gallon.

Edgar: Three dollars a gallon! That's double the normal price. No way! I can fill it myself! Give me back the keys …

Conversation B
Ten minutes later. Edgar's outside the airport. He's at a gas station.

Edgar: Where's the fuel cap lever? It isn't under the seat … Ah, here it is. What's wrong with this gas pump? It isn't working.

Driver: You have to pay in advance at this station.

Edgar: Oh, no! Look at the time.

Conversation C
Two minutes later.

Clerk: Good afternoon, sir. It's a great day, isn't it?

Edgar: I want to fill my car …

Clerk: How are you paying? Credit card or cash?

Edgar: Cash.

Clerk: Thirty dollars should be OK.

Edgar: Thirty? Twenty's enough … oh, it doesn't matter. There you go.

Clerk: Can I interest you in our new credit card? We …

Edgar: I don't have time for this.

1 👀 **It's five minutes later, and Edgar is collecting his change. Ask and answer.**

How much was the gas?
What coins and bills did Edgar get in his change?

2 👀 **Listen to all the Conversations. Ask the questions and answer with *Because* …**

a Why is Edgar in a hurry?
b Why doesn't Edgar want to pay $3 a gallon?
c Why does he want the keys back?
d Why couldn't Edgar find the fuel cap lever?
e Why isn't the gas pump working?

f Why doesn't Edgar want to hear about the new credit card?
g Why doesn't Edgar want the vouchers?

3 **Role-play the conversations. Change as many words as you can, e.g.**

The car's nearly full … does it matter?
price per liter NOT per gallon
different model of car
different amount of gas and change
You are interested in the credit card.
You don't want a receipt.
stamps not vouchers
free cassette tape with thirty stamps

51 Checking In

Conversation A
Edgar Young is at LAX.

Announcement: … and Flight CA 489 to
Vancouver is now leaving.
Edgar: Excuse me …
Man: Hey, bud. Stand in line like everyone else!
Edgar: But my flight's leaving …
Man: Aw, right. Go ahead.
Edgar: Thank you.

Conversation B

Check-in Clerk: May I have your ticket, sir?
Edgar: There you go.
Check-in Clerk: I'm sorry. This is a Coach Class
ticket. This is the Business Class check-in.
Edgar: But my flight's just leaving.
Check-in Clerk: Flight CA 489 to Vancouver? Yes,
I think you're too late.
Edgar: Oh, no! I have to be on it.
Check-in Clerk: Just a moment. Yes, you're OK.
I can check you in here.
Edgar: Thank goodness for that.
Check-in Clerk: Do you have any baggage?
Edgar: Yes. Two pieces.
Check-in Clerk: Did you pack the bags yourself?
Edgar: Yes, I did.
Check-in Clerk: Fine. Put them on the scales.

Conversation C

Edgar: I'd like an aisle seat, please.
Check-in Clerk: There are none left.
Edgar: Then I'd like a window seat.
Check-in Clerk: Sorry. The flight's nearly full.
There's a party of Sumo wrestlers going to
Vancouver. I only have a middle seat. OK?
Edgar: It's not between two Sumo wrestlers, is it?
Check in Clerk: Yes, it is. We tried to leave some
empty seats between them. The flight's boarding
now at Gate 35. Here's your boarding pass. Please
hurry. Have a good flight.

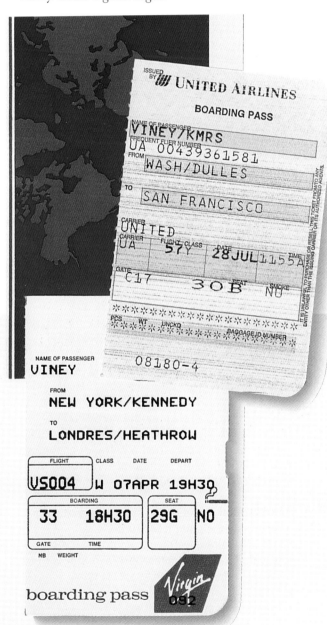

1 Look at Conversation A. Ask and answer.

a Why is the man angry with Edgar?
b Where do people stand in line in your country?
c Do people push into lines?
d Do other people get angry?

Standing in line

In the U.S.A. and Britain people don't push ahead in
lines. At post offices and banks there is often just one
line for several tellers. People wait in line and the first
person goes to the first free teller. The British word for
standing in line is "queuing". Teller means clerk.

**2 Look at these two boarding passes. One is
Washington to San Francisco. The other is New
York to London-Heathrow. Find this information:**

Airline / Flight number / Seat number / Departure
time / Gate number / Date / Smoking or non-
smoking

**3 Role-play conversations at check-in using the
boarding cards for information.**

52 Checking Out

Conversation A
Alicia is leaving the Columbia Towers Hotel.

Alicia: I'm checking out today. Here are my keys.
Pearl: Oh, really? We'll miss you. Did you enjoy your stay with us?
Alicia: Yes, I did. Very much.
Pearl: That's good. Where are you going now?
Alicia: I'm going on an Alaska Cruise. I'm going to take some pictures.
Pearl: Alaska? I'm sure you'll enjoy it.

Conversation B
Pearl: Did you have anything from the mini-bar last night?
Alicia: Yes. A small mineral water.
Pearl: Fine. I'll just print out your check. It won't take long.

Conversation C
Pearl: Do you want to just check this over?
Alicia: Thanks. Yes, everything's fine.
Pearl:: We have an imprint of your Visa card. Do you want to charge everything to Visa?
Alicia: Please.
Pearl: OK. Sign here. And here's a copy for your records. We hope you'll stay with us again.
Alicia: I will. And thank you for all your help.
Pearl: You're very welcome … er, did you complete your Guest Comments form?
Alicia: Oh, yes. There you go. Well, good-bye.
Pearl: Good-bye. Have a good trip.

1 **Conversation A. Role-play the conversation replacing the highlighted words, e.g.**
leaving / Here's my key card. / Was everything all right? / to Toronto / do some sightseeing

2 **Conversation B. Role-play the conversation replacing the highlighted words, e.g.**
three small whiskies / half a bottle of champagne / two mineral waters / a bar of chocolate / a pack of peanuts / It'll only take a moment.

3 **Conversation C. Role-play the conversation replacing the highlighted words, e.g.**
American Express / Do you want to put it all on your card? / Please come back and stay with us again. / Thanks for everything.

4 ★ **Communication Activities**
Student 1 – use Section H
Student 2 – use Section T

5 **Complete this mini-bar list for yourself for a weekend (or for Edgar Young). Interview a partner. What did they have from the mini-bar? Be careful with *a / an / some*.**

53 Your Cabin

Sunday, June 3. Alicia is on board the *Pacific Rim Voyager* at Canada Place. Maria, her cabin steward, is showing her to her cabin.

Maria: Right this way, Ms. Romero. This is your cabin.

Alicia: Thank you. It looks great.

Maria: This is the bathroom. You have a bath tub with a shower overhead.

Alicia: Fine.

Maria: And in the sitting area you have a TV.

Alicia: I won't have much time for TV. I'm here to work.

Maria: You mean, you aren't on vacation?

Alicia: Unfortunately not. I'm taking photographs for a travel brochure.

Maria: Oh, that's a pity.

Alicia: I'm looking forward to it. This is my first cruise.

Maria: Well, I hope you enjoy it.

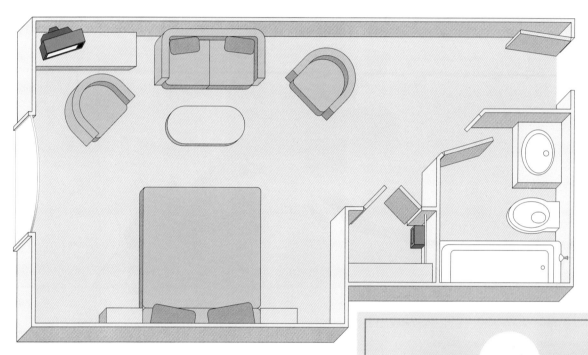

1 Role-play the conversation replacing the highlighted words, e.g.

shower cubicle / I'll be too busy to watch TV. / You mean you're here on business? / I think it'll be great. / I'm sure you'll enjoy it.

2 Look at the picture. What facilities does Alicia's cabin have? Check (✔) the boxes:

- ☐ queen-size bed
- ☐ dressing table
- ☐ writing desk
- ☐ walk-in closet
- ☐ laser disc player
- ☐ staircase
- ☐ sitting area
- ☐ dining table
- ☐ armchairs
- ☐ picture window
- ☐ balcony
- ☐ sofa
- ☐ shower
- ☐ TV

3 ◉◉ Look at the TV services card. Listen to Maria describing the facilities on the TV. Correct the mistakes on the card.

PACIFIC RIM CRUISES

THE PACIFIC RIM VOYAGER
TV SERVICES

CHANNEL	SERVICE
1	On-board information service
2	The movie channel – *2 hours a day*
3	Entertainment channel: *Adult programs 6 a.m. - 6 p.m.* *Kid's programs 6 p.m. - 11:30 p.m.*
4	Satellite – *NBC news*
5	Satellite – *Sports: table tennis, jogging*
6	Satellite – *Entertainment*
7	Satellite – *Old movies*
8	Charge account information – *interactive information on your account 24 hours a day*
9	Sega system video games – *control pads available from Entertainment desk*

Here is a postcard from Alaska.

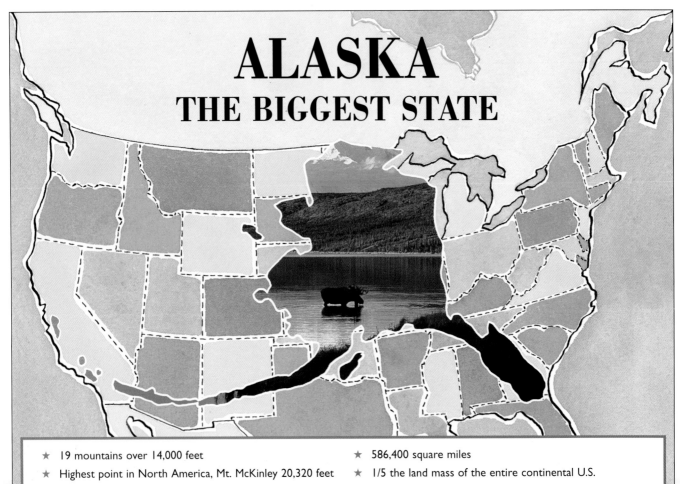

ALASKA
THE BIGGEST STATE

★ 19 mountains over 14,000 feet

★ Highest point in North America, Mt. McKinley 20,320 feet

★ More area than the 26 smallest states

★ Purchased from Russia in 1867 for less than 2¢ an acre

★ Longest days, 24 hours of daylight

★ Longest nights, 24 hours of night

★ More than 3 million lakes, larger than 25 acres

★ 586,400 square miles

★ 1/5 the land mass of the entire continental U.S.

★ More than two times the size of Texas

★ 29 active volcanoes, half the world's total

★ More coastline than the lower 48 states, 33,000 miles

★ More than half the world's glaciers

★ One glacier larger than Switzerland

1 Read the postcard, and find this information:

a the length of the coastline
b the height of the highest mountain
c the number of lakes
d the size of the largest glacier
e the price of the land when it was bought from Russia
f the date of the purchase
g the area of the state in square miles
h the percentage of the U.S. land mass covered by Alaska

2 Find the superlative forms of these adjectives:

long / high / low / large / small

3 Ask and answer about your country:

Which is the highest point?
How long are the longest days?
Which is the longest river?
Which is the largest lake?
Which is the biggest city?
Which is the largest state or province?
Is the biggest city also the capital?
What's the population?

55 Making Friends

Conversation A
Alicia is speaking to Josie on the cruise.

Josie: Hey, Alicia! Good to see you.

Alicia: Hello, er …

Josie: Josie Campbell? We met yesterday in Cecilia's office? We talked about photos of the excursions?

Alicia: Of course. You're the Excursions Manager.

Josie: That's right. Can I get you a drink?

Alicia: Please. A mineral water.

Josie: Are you sure? They have this new mineral water, Absolutely Arizona. I don't like it very much. It tastes very salty.

Alicia: OK. A club soda, then.

Conversation B

Josie: Is this your first trip to Alaska?

Alicia: Yes, it is. This is my first cruise, in fact.

Josie: What do you think of it so far?

Alicia: It's wonderful. It's a beautiful ship.

Josie: So you're enjoying yourself.

Alicia: Yes, but it feels a bit strange. I'm not really a passenger, and I'm not one of the ship's crew either.

Josie: OK, let me introduce you to some of the crew, then. Ken's over there. He's the Sports Manager. Come and meet him …

1 📟 **Conversation A. Alicia doesn't remember Josie at first. Listen to Josie's highlighted statements again – they sound like questions. Imagine Jack is speaking to someone who doesn't remember him. Try saying these sentences with question intonation:**

I'm Jack Hudson.
I'm from Phoenix.
I sell mineral water.
The brand's Absolutely Arizona.
We met last year.
We met at your office.
We had coffee.
I dropped my cup on your carpet.

Write a text about yourself. Introduce yourself to other students. You met them last year, but they can't remember you. Remind them who you are.

2 Conversation B. Josie asks about the trip to begin the conversation. Which of these topics is good for beginning a conversation?

the weather	food or drink
a trip	a hotel / hotel room
politics	the news

Think of a question for each of them and practice conversations.

3 Ask and answer, changing the words in parentheses.

What does (your soup) taste like?
What does (a piece of music) sound like?
How do (you) feel?
What does (fresh coffee) smell like?
What does (a famous place) look like?

Ken is in his office on board the *Pacific Rim Voyager*. Cecilia Grant is with him.

Kenji: Oh, no!

Cecilia: What's the matter?

Kenji: It's my computer! Look, there's coffee everywhere.

Cecilia: What happened?

Kenji: I knocked over my coffee cup. It went right over the keyboard.

Cecilia: Ken! You shouldn't put drinks near a computer.

Kenji: I know that! And all the information about the new sports program is on the computer. I don't have a back-up copy.

Cecilia: Oh, Ken. You should always back up important work.

Kenji: Well, I didn't. And I don't have a print-out either.

Cecilia: You can use my computer.

Kenji: Thanks. But there's hours of work here. I guess I'll have to start again.

Bramley Power 11500 Computer Manual

PRECAUTIONS

* **LIQUIDS!** Keep your computer away from liquids. Take care with beverages, and do not place the computer near an open window.

* **SAVE!** Always save work at regular intervals. Many programs have an auto-save facility.

* **BACK UP!** Always back up your work, either on floppy disks or other storage media.

* **CABLES!** Always turn off power before connecting or disconnecting any cables.

* **POWER!** Always use the shut-down command before turning off power.

* **~~FORCE!~~** Never force connectors into a port.

* **AIR VENTS!** Never put objects on top of the computer's air vents.

* **TRANSPORT!** Never transport the computer with discs in the floppy drive or CD-ROM drive.

1 Give Ken advice using the Precautions from the computer manual.

You should …

You shouldn't …

2 Are these computer commands the same in your country? Do you use these English words? If not, translate them.

QUIT	SAVE	OPEN	REPLACE
PRINT	FIND	CLOSE	CALCULATE
HELP	UNDO	SHUT DOWN	

3 ⊙⊙ Edgar Young is on a flight from Vancouver to Anchorage. Listen to the conversation. Ask and answer.

a Which things shouldn't you use on an airplane?

b Which airline does Edgar think he's flying on?

c Which airline is Edgar flying on?

⊙⊙ Listen again, and complete the blanks:

d You ____use your computer.

e I'm right in the ____of an important document.

f You'll ____to turn it off.

g It can interfere ____the airplane's equipment.

h I'll return it ____we get to Anchorage.

57 Skagway

SKAGWAY

Skagway has a permanent population of only 600, but 150,000 tourists visit it every year. The town is the nearest port to the Yukon territory of Canada, and gold was discovered in the Klondike area of Yukon in 1896. A year later the world heard the news when the steamship *Portland* arrived in Seattle with its famous "ton of gold". Twelve days later the first of hundreds of steamships arrived in Skagway. By 1898 the population of Skagway was nearly 20,000. It had fifteen general stores, nineteen restaurants, eleven saloons, nine hotels, and four newspapers. Gold miners walked over the dangerous White Pass in freezing snow to get to the gold fields. Many died.

THE PACIFIC RIM VOYAGER EXCURSIONS:
WEDNESDAY JUNE 6th, 8 A.M.– 3 P.M.

EXCURSION 6/01
Ride the White Pass & Yukon Railroad. The railroad opened in 1900. You ride in genuine 1900s parlor cars!

EXCURSION 6/03
Enjoy 4WD vehicle sightseeing around Skagway and up the Klondike Highway to the White Pass Summit.

EXCURSION 6/02
Glacier flightseeing. Helicopter trip to a glacier. Land on a glacier with experienced guides. The thrill of a lifetime!

Or just stay in town for the best souvenir shopping in Alaska!

1 Ask and answer.
  a When was gold discovered in the Klondike?
  b When did people first know about this?
  c When did the first gold miners' ships arrive in Skagway?
  d How did the first miners get to the Yukon?
  e Describe Skagway in 1898.
  f Describe the picture of Skagway today.

2 Read about the excursions. Which excursion would you like to take? Why?

3 ★ Communication Activities
Student 1 – use Section I
Student 2 – use Section R

4 Look at the excursions program. Alicia wants to take as many photos as she can for the brochure. Which excursion should Alicia take? Why? Suggest three excursions from your town, and write ads for them.

58 Souvenirs

Conversation A
Ketchikan, Alaska. Alicia Romero is shopping for souvenirs.

Assistant: May I help you?
Alicia: No, thanks. I'm just looking.
Assistant: Well, take your time. Please ask me if you need any information.
Alicia: I will. Thank you.

Conversation B
Alicia: These blankets are really beautiful.
Assistant: Yes, they are. They're all genuine Native American designs, made of pure wool, and they're made here in Alaska.
Alicia: I need some throws for my apartment … but I need more than one.
Assistant: How many do you need?
Alicia: Two, maybe three.
Assistant: Well, they're $95 each, but I can give you a discount on three.
Alicia: Really? How much?
Assistant: $250 for the three.
Alicia: Hmm. I don't have much space in my cabin.
Assistant: We can ship them anywhere in the United States.
Alicia: San Diego?
Assistant: Sure. That's no problem.
Alicia: They're really nice … but I don't know.
Assistant: We won't charge you for shipping.
Alicia: OK. It's a deal. Do you take American Express?

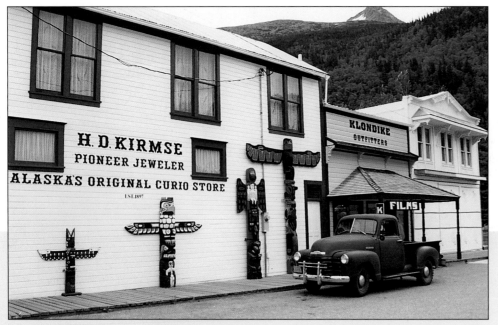

$195

$95

$16.95

$5.99

$19.99

1 **You are looking for presents for friends and relations. Ask and answer in pairs, e.g.**

What would your sister like?
My sister would like a T-shirt.

2 ★ **Communication Activities. Role-play a dialog in the shop. You want several of each item. Try to negotiate a discount. Ask about shipping charges. Each item will go to a different address. The shop assistant should turn to Section V.**

3 **Ask and answer.**

Do shops in your country generally have fixed prices, or can you bargain?
What kind of shops can you bargain in?
Can you get a discount for cash payments?

Do shops charge you for shipping?
Do you buy things mail order from catalogs?
Are they cheaper or more expensive?

59 Good News

Conversation A
Ken is in the gym on the *Pacific Rim Voyager*.

Syreeta: Ken? There's a phone call for you.
Kenji: Not now, Syreeta. I'm going to take a shower.
Syreeta: Uh, Ken … it's important.
Kenji: Ask them to call back in twenty minutes.
Syreeta: Ken … it's Michael Perez.
Kenji: Perez? The VP in charge of operations? What does he want?
Syreeta: Nothing bad, I hope!

Conversation B

Kenji: Mr. Perez? This is Ken Nakamura speaking … Sorry, Mr. Perez, I was coaching some passengers … Yes, I know Paul O'Connell. He's the Entertainment Director on the *Pacific Rim Explorer* … Oh, dear. I'm sorry to hear that. How is he? … Good, it's not serious then … Oh, I see. Six months? … Yes, we're going to be in Vancouver on Sunday … Sorry, can you say that again? … Well, thank you. Thank you very much … Yes, sure, I'll take it … Uh, who's going to tell Cecilia Grant? … Right. She knows already … Yes, Syreeta will be great … Yes, I'll tell her right now … Good-bye, sir.
Syreeta: Fascinating. What was that all about?
Kenji: Syreeta, I have some good news for you … and for me!

---

1 Look at Conversation A. Use the charts below, and practice the conversation replacing the highlighted expressions.

Not now	I'm just going to	take a shower.
Not at the moment	I have to	finish something.
Later	I need to	speak to someone first.
I can't stop now.	I want to	get some information first.

2 ☺☺ Look at Conversation B. Listen to Ken's conversation. Can you guess what Michael Perez is saying? Think about it, and write down some ideas. Then role-play the conversation.

Ask	them / her	to call back / me	in	20 minutes / half an hour.
Tell	him / the caller	to call / try again	at	twelve thirty / four o'clock.

3 ☺☺ Listen to Ken's conversation again. This time you can hear Michael Perez too. Compare the conversation with your guesses.

4 Answer the questions:
  a What happened to Paul O'Connell?
  b How long is he going to be away from work?
  c What was Paul's job?
  d When is Ken going to be in Vancouver?
  e What's Ken's new job?
  f What's Syreeta's new job?

5 Role-play Syreeta and Ken. Give Syreeta the good news.

60 Good-Bye

Conversation A
The ship is back in Vancouver. It's the end of the cruise.
Alicia: Well, good-bye, Josie. And thanks for everything.
Josie: Good-bye. It was nice meeting you.
Alicia: Don't forget. You have my address. Call me next time you're in San Diego.
Josie: I will. And call me if you're ever in Vancouver.
Alicia: OK. Good-bye, then.
Josie: Good-bye. Take care.

Conversation B
Cecilia: Ken, I want to thank you for all your hard work.

Kenji: Thank <u>you</u>, Cecilia. I'm sorry that I'm leaving. It was good working with you.
Cecilia: Thanks. It's quite a surprise, but it's a good promotion for you. You deserve it.
Kenji: It was a surprise for me, too.
Cecilia: You'll be great. Enjoy the job.
Kenji: And thanks again for suggesting me.

Conversation C
Josie: So, you're moving to the *Pacific Rim Explorer*. Good luck.
Kenji: Thanks. Er … I'm going to miss you, Josie.
Josie: And I'll miss you. Keep in touch.
Kenji: Sure. I'll call you … if that's OK.
Josie: Yes, I'll look forward to it. Uh, good-bye then.
Kenji: Good-bye.

LANGUAGE BANK		
Thanks before good-byes:		
Thanks	for	everything.
Thank you		(all) your help.
Thank you very much		(all) your hard work.
I want to thank you		(all) your kindness.
I'd like to thank you		(all) your assistance.

Adding something after good-bye:

Take care.	Keep in touch.
Look after yourself.	Keep in contact.
Enjoy (the job).	Call me.

1 Role-play conversations using the Language Bank.
- Alicia saying good-bye to Cecilia.
- Ken saying good-bye to Alicia.
- A passenger saying good-bye to another passenger after a shipboard romance!

2 👀 What's going to happen to everyone? Listen to some possibilities. Can you continue the story?

3 ★ Communication Activities
So, do you prefer a happy ending or an unhappy ending to the story?
Student 1 – use Section K
Student 2 – use Section U

Grammar Reference

SURVIVAL FILES

indefinite articles

definite articles / demonstratives

to be

have

pronouns / possessive adjectives

imperatives

adjectives

adverbs

quantity

present continuous

likes and dislikes

present simple

was and *were*

past simple

going to future

'll future

comparison

location and movement

modals

Irregular verbs, past tense

VOCABULARY FILES

numbers

days and dates

countries and nationalities

weights and measures

money

colors

time

SURVIVAL FILE 1: *indefinite articles*

indefinite articles – *a / an*

Use **a** before the sound of consonants (b/c/d/f/g/h/j/k/l/m/n/p/q/r/s/t/v/w/x/y/z):
a book / a computer / a disk / a flight / a good grade / a jeans shop, etc.

Use **an** before the sound of vowels (a/e/i/o/u):
an Apple computer / an exit / an idea / an operating system / an umbrella

The indefinite article agrees with the next word, not with the next noun:
an open book / a long inquiry / a few oranges / an easy exercise

Remember:
Some consonants are silent, or the sound is a vowel sound:
an honest answer / 30 miles an hour / an MD / an HD computer disk / an x-ray
(consonant capital letters with a vowel sound are F, H, L, M, N, R, S, X)

Often **u / eu** have a **y** consonant sound at the beginning of a word:
a university / a United Airlines ticket / a U.S. Senator / a European diplomat / a Euro

We use **a / an** for jobs and categories:
*She's **an** engineer* not ~~She's engineer.~~

*He's **an** officer.*
*Are you **a** student?*
*A turkey is **a** bird.*
*A guitar is **a** musical instrument.*

SURVIVAL FILE 2: *definite articles /demonstratives*

definite articles

*Give me **a** blue pen.*
(There are several pens. Three are blue. Give me any of the blue pens.)
*Give me **the** blue pen.*
(There is only one blue pen. Give it to me.)

*It's on **the** second floor.*
*Cecilia Grant is **the** manager of the department.*
*Where's **the** rest room?*

We always say:
the sun / **the** Earth / **the** ocean
the police / **the** air force
play **the** guitar / play **the** piano

the: for places
We do not use **the** for most place names:
Costa Rica is in Central America.
Los Angeles is a city in California.
Their office is on Highland Avenue.
They have an office downtown.
The flight leaves from Kennedy Airport.
Union Street Station is right over there.
San Diego Zoo is famous.

We use **the** for:
the names of oceans, rivers, important buildings, hotels, restaurants, boats, etc.:
The *Pacific Ocean /* **The** *Panama Canal /* **The** *Colorado River /* **The** *CN Tower /* **The** *Smithsonian Museum /* **The** *Pleasure Island Ten Movie Theater /* **The** *Four Seasons Hotel /* **The** *Panama Hat Restaurant /* **The** *Pacific Rim Voyager*

the official names of some countries / states – especially with *of*:
The *United States of America /* **The** *United Kingdom /* **The** *Province of Ontario /* **The** *State of Oregon*

other place / company names with *of*:
The *Bank of America /* **The** *coast of Texas /* **The** *west of Canada*

plural names of countries and places:
The *Philippines /* **The** *Netherlands /* **The** *Rocky Mountains /* **The** *Aleutian Islands /* **The** *South Pole*

demonstratives

this, that, these, and ***those*** are demonstratives.

	singular	plural
near (here)	this	these
far (there)	that	those

SURVIVAL FILE 3: *to be*

I	am	busy.
	'm	here.
	'm not	tired.
	am not	a student.
He	is	American.
She	's	
It	isn't	
	's not	
	is not	
We	are	
You	're	
They	aren't	
	're not	
	are not	

Am	I	busy?
Is	he	here?
Isn't	she	tired?
	it	a student?
Are	you	American?
Aren't	we	
	they	

Yes,	I	am.
	you	are.
	we	
	they	
	he	is.
	she	
	it	

No,	I	'm not.
	you	aren't.
	we	
	they	
	he	isn't.
	she	
	it	

Infinitive: *to be*
Present Participle: *being*
Past Participle: *been*

Note: for past tense, see *was / were* below

SURVIVAL FILE 4: *have*

I	have	a car.
You	have got	some money.
We	've got	a pen.
They	don't have	two brothers.
	haven't got	
He	has	
She	has got	
It	's got	
	doesn't have	
	hasn't got	

Do	I	have	a car?
Don't	you		any money?
	we		a pen?
	they		any brothers?
Does	he		
Doesn't	she		
	it		

or

Have	I	got	a car?
Haven't	you		any money?
	we		a pen?
	they		any brothers?
Has	he		
Hasn't	she		
	it		

Yes,	I	do.
	you	
	we	
	they	
	he	does.
	she	
	it	

No,	I	don't.
	you	do not.
	we	
	they	
	he	doesn't.
	she	does not.
	it	

or

Yes,	I	have.
	you	
	we	
	they	
	he	has.
	she	
	it	

No,	I	haven't.
	you	
	we	
	they	
	he	hasn't.
	she	
	it	

have / have got

have / has / don't have / doesn't have + Do you have ...? / Does she have ...? is <u>more common</u> in American English.

have got / has got / haven't got / hasn't got + Have you got ...? / Has he got ...? is <u>more common</u> in British English.

Note: <u>but</u> both forms are used and understood in both the U.S.A. and in Britain.
In the U.S.A. *have got / has got / haven't got*, etc. is common, but many people think it isn't "good English" and prefer *have / don't have*

In Britain *have / don't have* is becoming more popular (because of American TV and movies). Some people think it "sounds more polite". But *have got / haven't got* is the normal everyday form.

If you ask questions with *Have you got ...? / Has she got ...?*, answer with *Yes, I have / No, I haven't.*

If you ask questions with *Do you have ...? / Does he have ...?*, answer with *Yes, I do / No, I don't.*

In the U.S.A. you can hear mixed examples. Understand them, but don't imitate them: *Have you got the time? Yes, I do. It's 12:30.*
In fact, spoken American and British English, *Have you got ...?* often sounds like *You got ...?*

SURVIVAL FILE 5: *pronouns/possessive adjectives*

subject pronoun	object pronoun	possessive pronoun	reflexive pronoun
I	me	my	myself
you	you	your	yourself
he	him	his	himself
she	her	her	herself
it	it	its	itself
we	us	our	ourselves
you	you	your	yourselves
they	them	their	themselves

1. subject pronoun

I don't like her. / **She** doesn't like me. / **We**'re working hard.

2. object pronoun

Give it to **me**. / Look at **them**. / He's talking to **her**.

3. possessive adjective

It's **his** book. / **My** uncle lives in L.A. / **Our** class is small.

4. reflexive pronoun

Help **yourselves** to salad. / Get **yourself** a plate.

5. indefinite pronouns

affirmative	negative	question
someone	no one / not … anyone	anyone?
somebody	nobody / not … anybody	anybody?
somewhere	nowhere / not … anywhere	anywhere?
something	nothing / not … anything	anything?

There's **someone** at the door. Who is it?
Is there **anything** in the fridge? I'm really hungry.
It's a small town **somewhere** near Seattle.

SURVIVAL FILE 6: *imperatives*

We use the imperative to give instructions, to give orders, to make offers, suggestions, and requests.

The imperative is the same as the infinitive without *to:*
Come here.
Listen.
Look at this.
Press this button.
Take a right.
Give me that book.
Enjoy your meal.

the negative
Don't talk.
Don't worry.
Don't press that button.
Don't turn left, turn right.

Signs use *do not:*
DO NOT PARK HERE
DO NOT STOP

the verb *to be*
Be careful.
Be quiet.
Don't **be** stupid.

emphatic uses
We can emphasize an imperative with *do:*
Please, sit down.
(stronger) Please, **do** sit down.
Be quiet.
(stronger) **Do** be quiet!
Close that door.
(stronger) **Do** close that door!

Adjectives come before the noun:

It's a **big** ship.

He's a **tall** guy with glasses.

Can I have the **blue** pen, please?

Adjectives do not change their endings:

an **old** car / an **old** man / an **old** woman

an **old** book / some **old** books / **old** people

to be **+ adjective**

They're **American.**

It's **cold.**

I'm **tired.**

Are you **busy**?

verbs of perception + adjective

I feel **hot.**

You look **tired.**

They seem **happy.**

We feel **great.**

It tastes **strange.**

He sounds **interesting.**

She looks **Spanish.**

They smell **wonderful.**

frequency adverbs

1. position with the present simple

I	always	get up early.
You	usually	take a train to work.
We	generally	
They	often	
He	sometimes	gets up early.
She	hardly ever	takes a train to work.
It	never	

2. with negatives

I don't **often** go there.

She doesn't **usually** arrive late for work.

3. position with *to be*

I	am	always	busy.
	'm	usually	here.
He	is	generally	tired.
She	's	often	
It		sometimes	
We	are	hardly ever	
You	're	never	
They			

4. questions

How **often** do you do that?

Do you **ever** (drink hot chocolate)?

Do you **usually** (wear that tie to work)?

adverbs

Ken's a **good** tennis player. He plays tennis **well.**

good is an adjective (it answers the question "What kind of **player** is he?")

well is an adverb (it answers the question "How does he **play**?")

We use an **adverb of manner** to tell us more about a verb (How?):

*She's running **quickly**.*

We use an adverb as a **modifier** for an adjective:

*It's a **very** interesting book.*

*It's a **really** difficult question.*

*That's a **pretty** good answer.*

Most **adverbs of manner** have the regular ending -ly:

adjective	quick	slow	careful	angry	nice	bad
adverb	quickly	slowly	carefully	angrily	nicely	badly

Some frequent adverbs are irregular:

adjective	good	fast	hard
adverb	well	fast	hard

Some adverbs have a regular form and an irregular form. Examples are **real / really** and **slow / slowly**

In written English, use the regular form:

*It's a **really** difficult question.*

*The car goes **slowly**.*

In everyday spoken English, the irregular form is common:

*It's a **real** good burger bar.*

*That car goes **slow**.*

SURVIVAL FILE 9: *quantity*

1. uncountable nouns and countable nouns

English nouns are in two groups.

uncountable nouns: water, gas, cheese, butter, oil, time, energy, space

countable nouns: books, cars, kilobytes, liters of water, minutes, hours, kilowatts

Uncountable nouns take a singular verb:
*There **is** some water.*
*There **wasn't** any wine.*
*There **isn't** any time.*
*How much milk **is** there?*

Countable nouns take a plural verb:
*There **are** some bread rolls.*
*There **weren't** any cookies.*
*There **aren't** any glasses.*
*How many people **are** there at the party?*

Note: we can't count water, cheese, or time, but we can count liters or gallons (of water), bottles (of water), pounds or kilos (of cheese), packs (of cheese), minutes, hours, and seconds.

2. some / any

affirmative

some:	*There is **some** water. / There are **some** glasses.*

negative

no / not ... any	*There's **no** water. / There is**n't** **any** water.*
	*There are **no** glasses. / There are**n't** **any** glasses.*

question

any	*Is there **any** water? Are there **any** glasses?*

3. How much? How many?

We use **How much** for uncountables: ***How much** water is there?*
We use **How many** for countables: ***How many** glasses are there?*

We also use **How much** for prices:
***How much** is that bottled water? It's 99¢ a bottle.*
***How much** are those glasses? They're $3.50 each.*

4. a lot of / lots of / a little / a few

We use **a lot of** or **lots of** for countable and uncountable nouns:
*There's **a lot of** water./ There's **lots of** water.*
*There are **a lot of** glasses. / There are **lots of** glasses.*

We use **a little** for uncountables: *There's (only) **a little** water.*
We use a **few** for countables: *There are (only) **a few** glasses.*

SURVIVAL FILE 10: *present continuous*

I	am	working	now.
	'm		right now.
	'm not		at the moment.
	am not		at this time.
He	is		
She	's		
It	isn't		
	's not		
	is not		
We	are		
You	're		
They	aren't		
	're not		
	are not		

Am	I	working	now?
			right now?
			at the moment?
			at this time?
Is	he		
Isn't	she		
	it		
Are	you		
Aren't	we		
	they		

Yes,	I	am.
	you	are.
	we	
	they	
	he	is.
	she	
	it	

No,	I	'm not.
	you	aren't.
	we	
	they	
	he	isn't.
	she	
	it	

1. questions

What are you doing?
Where is he going?
Who is she talking to?
When is it coming?
Why am I feeling tired?

2. present continuous + object

I'm eating ice cream.
We're watching a program on TV.
He's driving a new car.
They're playing golf.

3. present continuous future

We use the present continuous for future plans and appointments:

I'm meeting with them tomorrow.
She's going to the bank on Tuesday.
We're seeing our friends this evening at 8:30.
He isn't visiting us next week.

What are you doing tomorrow / on Saturday / next summer?

I	like	tea.
You	enjoy	football.
We	don't like	swimming.
They	don't enjoy	work.
He	likes	opera.
She	enjoys	
It	doesn't like	
	doesn't enjoy	

Do	I	like	tea?
Don't	you	enjoy	football?
	we		swimming?
	they		work?
Does	he		opera?
Doesn't	she		
	it		

Yes,	I	do.
	you	
	we	
	they	
	he	does.
	she	
	it	

No,	I	don't.
	you	do not.
	we	
	they	
	he	doesn't.
	she	does not.
	it	

1. like doing

We say 'I like swimming' NOT ~~I like swim / I like to swim.~~

2. other verbs for likes and dislikes

love   hate
like   dislike

These verbs are usually in the **present simple** form, not the **present continuous**
We do not say: ~~I am liking …~~ or ~~I am hating …~~

3. similar verbs

These are examples of verbs which are also usually in the **present simple** form, not the
present continuous:

want   need
understand   think
know   hope

4. enjoy can be in the present simple or present continuous

Habit: Do you enjoy TV programs about crime?
Now: Are you enjoying the movie?

I	go to work	every day.
You	have a shower	in the morning.
We	don't go to work	at 7 o'clock.
They	don't take a shower	early.
He	goes to work	
She	takes a shower	
It	doesn't go to work	
	doesn't take a shower	

Do	I	go to work	every day?
Don't	you	takes a shower	in the morning?
	we		at 7 o'clock?
	they		early?
Does	he		
Doesn't	she		
	it		

Yes,	I	do.
	you	
	we	
	they	
	he	does.
	she	
	it	

No,	I	don't.
	you	do not.
	we	
	they	
	he	doesn't.
	she	does not.
	it	

1. Questions

What do you do?
Where do they live?
When does he start work?
Who does she know?

2. Present simple time words

I finish work **at** 6 o'clock / 7:30.
I don't work **on** Sundays / Tuesdays.
We don't work **in** the evening / morning.
It doesn't snow **in** summer / July.
She drives **to** the city every day.
They **often** play tennis.

SURVIVAL FILE 13: *was and were*

was and **were** are the past simple of *to be*:

I	was	late	yesterday.
He	wasn't	there	at 9 o'clock.
She			last week.
It			last month.
We	were		last Monday.
You	weren't		in 1995.
They			

Was	I	late	yesterday?
Wasn't	he	there	at 9 o'clock?
	she		last week?
	it		last month?
Were	you		last Monday?
Weren't	we		in 1995?
	they		

Yes,	I	was.
	he	
	she	
	it	
	you	were.
	we	
	they	

No,	I	wasn't.
	he	
	she	
	it	
	you	weren't.
	we	
	they	

1. Questions

When **were** you in America?
What time **was** your flight?
Who **were** you with?

2. Past continuous

See Present continuous above.
was / were + present participle:

I **was waiting** for a bus.
She **was wearing** a blue jacket.
We **were living** in France (when it happened).
They **were watching** TV (when the phone rang)
What **were** you **doing**?
Where **was** she **staying**?

SURVIVAL FILE 14: *past simple*

I	had	a good	flight.
You	didn't have	a bad	trip.
He		a long	journey.
She		a boring	drive.
It		a tiring	ride.
We			
They			

Did	I	have	a good	flight?
	you		a bad	trip?
	we		a long	journey?
	they		a boring	drive?
	he		a tiring	ride?
	she			
	it			

Yes, I did.
Yes, she did.

No, I didn't.
No, he didn't.

1. Regular verbs

Regular verbs end with -ed in the affirmative past simple. Look at the spelling:

+ed	+d	+ y >>> ied
walk / walked	like / liked	hurry / hurried
want / wanted	love / loved	worry / worried
need / needed	inquire / inquired	supply / supplied

2. Irregular verbs

Many common verbs are irregular. Examples:

buy / bought	go / went	say / said
come / came	have / had	see / saw
do / did	know / knew	take / took
fly / flew	meet / met	write / wrote

I	am	going to	be there	tomorrow.
	'm		do it	at 3:30.
	'm not		see you	on Thursday.
	am not			in August.
He	is			next week.
She	's			next month.
It	isn't			next winter.
	's not			next year.
	is not			in 2006.
We	are			
You	're			
They	aren't			
	're not			
	are not			

Yes,	I	am.		No,	I	'm not.
	you	are.			you	aren't.
	we				we	
	they				they	
	he	is.			he	isn't.
	she				she	
	it				it	

Questions

What are you going to do?
Where is she going to go?
Who is he going to meet?
When are they going to meet?

Am	I	going to	be there	tomorrow?
			do it	at 3:30?
			see you	on Thursday?
Are	you			in August?
Aren't	we			next week?
	they			next month?
Is	he			next winter?
Isn't	she			next year?
	it			in 2006?

I	'll	be there	tomorrow.	Will	I	be there	tomorrow?	Yes,	I	will.		No,	I	won't.
He	will	do it	at 9 o'clock.	Won't	he	do it	at 9 o'clock?		you				you	
She	won't	see you	next week.		she	see you	next week?		we				we	
It	will not		next month.		it		next month?		they				they	
We			next year.		you		next year?		he				he	
You			next Friday.		we		next Friday?		she				she	
They			in 2003.		they		in 2003?		it				it	

1. non-future meanings

The 'll future is often used for "non-future" meanings:

offers: I'll get you a drink.
requests: Will you open the door?
promises: I'll send the information by fax.

2. shall

In British English you use **shall** for first person questions (I and we):
suggestions: Shall we have something to eat?
offers: Shall I get you a drink?
You cannot use **will** in these examples.

In very formal British and American English **shall** can be used for affirmatives also.
In British English, there is also the negative form **shan't**. In American English this is always **shall not**.

Shall is used for legal documents and orders in both Britain and America. The meaning is stronger than **will**, it really means **must**:
All soldiers **shall** have short hair.
The President **shall** report to Congress.
See also the famous American Civil Rights song "We **Shall** Overcome" and the gospel song "We **Shall** Not Be Moved".

SURVIVAL FILE 17: *comparison*

	adjective	comparative	superlative
shorter adjectives	fast	faster	the fastest
	slow	slower	the slowest
	big	bigger	the biggest
	happy	happier	the happiest
irregular	good	better	the best
	bad	worse	the worst
long adjective (+)	important	more important	the most important
	expensive	more expensive	the most expensive
long adjectives (−)	important	less important	the least important
	expensive	less expensive	the least expensive

1. comparatives

Don't forget **than**:

*This one is bigger **than** that one.*
*The blue one is less expensive **than** the green one.*
*She's better at tennis **than** he is.*

2. superlatives

In formal grammar, we use comparatives for two things, superlatives for three or more things:

*There are two of them. They are both good, but this one is **better**.*
*There are (six) of them. They are all good, but this one's **the best**.*

In spoken English, people are using superlatives more and more for only two things:

*Look at your book and my book. My book's **the oldest**.*

Remember! When you are comparing two things with **than**, you must use the comparative!

*Look at your book and my book. My book's **older than** your book.*

3. comparatives: (not) as ... as ...

*I'm **as** tall **as** my father.*
*My book isn't **as** new **as** your book.*
*It's not **as** difficult **as** it looks.*

SURVIVAL FILE 18: *location and movement*

next to / beside   in   on   under

above   below   behind   in front of

opposite   in between   near   into

out of / from   through   across   along

I	can	be there	right now.
He	can't	do it	every day.
She	should	see you	tomorrow.
It	shouldn't		at 9 o'clock.
We	would		next year.
You	wouldn't		next Friday.
They	may		in 2003.
	might		
	might not		
	must		
	mustn't		

Can	I	be there	right now?
Should	he	do it	every day?
Would	she	see you	tomorrow?
Might	it		at 9 o'clock?
Must	you		next year?
	we		next Friday?
	they		in 2003?

Yes,	I	can.
	he	should.
	she	would.
	it	might.
	you	must.
	we	
	they	

No.	I	can't.
	he	shouldn't.
	she	wouldn't.
	it	might not.
	you	mustn't.
	we	needn't.
	they	

can / cannot for ability and permission:
I can swim. / He can't dance. / Can I leave?

should for advice and obligation:
You should always back up your work on disk.
You shouldn't drive so fast!

would for requests and offers:
I'd like a cup of coffee, please.
Would you like my address?

might and **may** for possibility and permission:
May I help you?
May I leave the room?
It may rain tomorrow.
I might be in Phoenix in July.

must / mustn't for very strong obligation:
You must be here by 9 o'clock.
You mustn't smoke in public places in California.

needn't when there is no obligation:
You needn't finish that work now. You can do it tomorrow.

present	past simple
am / is / are	was / were
begin	began
bring	brought
buy	bought
come	came
cost	cost
do / does	did
drink	drank
drive	drove
eat	ate
fall	fell
find	found
fly	flew
forget	forgot
get	got
give	gave
go	went
has / have	had
hear	heard
hold	held
keep	kept

present	past simple
know	knew
leave	left
lose	lost
make	made
mean	meant
pay	paid
put	put
say	said
see	saw
sell	sold
send	sent
shut	shut
sit	sat
speak	spoke
spend	spent
take	took
teach	taught
tell	told
think	thought
understand	understood
write	wrote

VOCABULARY FILE 1: *numbers*

1 – one	11 – eleven	21 – twenty-one	40 – forty	1000 – one thousand
2 – two	12 – twelve	22 – twenty-two	50 – fifty	10,000 – ten thousand
3 – three	13 – thirteen	23 – twenty-three	60 – sixty	100,000 – one hundred thousand
4 – four	14 – fourteen	24 – twenty-four	70 – seventy	1,000,000 – one million
5 – five	15 – fifteen	25 – twenty-five	80 – eighty	
6 – six	16 – sixteen	26 – twenty-six	90 – ninety	
7 – seven	17 – seventeen	27 – twenty-seven	100 – one hundred / a hundred	
8 – eight	18 – eighteen	28 – twenty-eight	101 – one hundred and one	
9 – nine	19 – nineteen	29 – twenty-nine	122 – one hundred and twenty-two	
10 – ten	20 – twenty	30 – thirty	659 – six hundred and fifty-nine	

VOCABULARY FILE 2: *days and dates*

Days of the week

Monday
Tuesday
Wednesday
Thursday
Friday
Saturday
Sunday

Months of the year

January	July
February	August
March	September
April	October
May	November
June	December

Years

1996 … nineteen ninety-six
1900 … nineteen hundred
1905 … nineteen hundred and five / nineteen "oh" five
2000 … two thousand
2001 … two thousand and one / twenty "oh" one
2067 … twenty sixty-seven

Ordinal Numbers for Dates

1st … first	7th … seventh	13th … thirteenth	19th … nineteenth	25th … twenty-fifth
2nd … second	8th … eighth	14th … fourteenth	20th … twentieth	26th … twenty-sixth
3rd … third	9th … ninth	15th … fifteenth	21st … twenty-first	27th … twenty-seventh
4th … fourth	10th … tenth	16th … sixteenth	22nd … twenty-second	28th … twenty-eighth
5th … fifth	11th … eleventh	17th … seventeenth	23rd … twenty-third	29th … twenty-ninth
6th … sixth	12th … twelfth	18th … eighteenth	24th … twenty-fourth	30th … thirtieth

VOCABULARY FILE 3: *countries and nationalities*

ending with -an

Chile	Chilean
Germany	German
Korea	Korean
Mexico	Mexican
Singapore	Singaporean
United States of America	American
Venezuela	Venezuelan

ending with -ese

Burma	Burmese
China	Chinese
Japan	Japanese
Portugal	Portuguese
Taiwan	Taiwanese
Vietnam	Vietnamese

ending in -i

Israel	Israeli
Kuwait	Kuwaiti
Iraq	Iraqi
Pakistan	Pakistani
Saudi Arabia	Saudi

ending with -ian

Australia	Australian
Argentina	Argentinian
Brazil	Brazilian
Canada	Canadian
Colombia	Colombian
Hungary	Hungarian
India	Indian
Indonesia	Indonesian
Italy	Italian
Malaysia	Malaysian
Russia	Russian

ending with -ish

Britain	British
Denmark	Danish
England	English
Ireland	Irish
Poland	Polish
Scotland	Scottish
Spain	Spanish
Sweden	Swedish

others

Czech Republic	Czech
France	French
Greece	Greek
Netherlands (Holland)	Dutch
New Zealand	New Zealand (adjective), a New Zealander (person)
Philippines	Filipino
Switzerland	Swiss
Thailand	Thai

In this section we are using the international spellings: "litre", "metre", etc.

The U.S.A. does not use the metric system.
When Americans write metric measures, they use different spelling for "meter" and "liter".
Canada and Australia use the metric system. Road signs are in kilometres. Weights are in grams / kilograms. Gasoline is sold in litres. Temperatures are in degrees Celsius (or Centigrade).

Britain is changing to the metric system. Older people still use non-metric ("Imperial") weights and measures. Schools began teaching metric measurements in the early 1970s (and stopped teaching Imperial measurements at the same time).
Petrol (U.S. – gasoline) is sold in litres.
Since 1995 all shops must use metric weights.
BUT miles are still used for distances and road signs.
In conversation, Fahrenheit temperatures are often used.

Length

one mile = 1.609 kilometres
one kilometre = 0.6214 miles
one metre = 1.094 yards
one yard = 0.914 metres
one centimetre = 0.394 inches
one inch = 25.4 millimetres / 2.54 centimetres
There are 12 inches in one foot, three feet in one yard.

Approximations:
You can think of 5 kilometres = 3 miles
You can think of one metre = 1 yard
You can think of 30 cm = 1 foot

Weights

one kilogram = 2.205 pounds
one pound = 0.454 kilograms
one ton = 1016.04 kilograms

Approximations:
You can think of 1 kilo = 2 pounds
You can think of one pound = half a kilo
You can think of 1 ton = 1 tonne (metric)

Capacity (e.g. gasoline, water)

There is a problem here. The U.S.A. and Britain have different measurements for a pint and a gallon. We say "U.S. gallon" and "Imperial gallon" and "U.S. pint" and "Imperial pint" if we want to note the difference. There are eight pints in a gallon. Two gallons are a quart. In the U.S.A. milk and alcohol are often sold in quarts. Remember that Britain now officially does not use Imperial measures.

one litre = 2.1 U.S. pints / 1.76 Imperial pints
one U.S. pint = 0.473 litres
one Imperial pint = 0.568 litres
one U.S. gallon = 3.785 litres
one Imperial gallon = 4.546 litres

Approximations (for U.S. and Imperial systems):

You can think of one quart = 1 litre.
You can think of two pints = 1 litre.
You can think of two gallons = 8 (U.S.A.) or 9 (U.K.) litres.

Temperature

The Celsius (or Centigrade) system is used everywhere for scientific measurements.
The U.S.A. uses the Fahrenheit system in conversation.
Canada and Britain officially use the Celsius system.
In Britain you can hear people talk about weather temperatures in Fahrenheit, but TV weather forecasts are in Celsius.

	°C	°F
water freezes (becomes ice)	0°C	32°F
a cool day, wear a coat	7°C	45°F
a mild day	15°C	59°F
pleasant office temperature	22°C	72°C
a hot day for the beach	30°C	86°F
the temperature of the human body	37°C	98.6°F
water boils (becomes steam)	100°C	212°F
cooking temperature in an oven	220°C	425°F

VOCABULARY FILE 5: *money*

United States of America

One dollar = 100 cents
Coins:
1¢ (penny), 5¢ (nickel), 10¢ (dime),
25¢ (quarter)
Bills:
$1, $5, $10, $20, $50, $100

Canada

One dollar = 100 cents
Coins:
1¢ (penny), 5¢ (nickel), 10¢ (dime),
25¢ (quarter), $1
Bills:
$2, $5, $10, $20, $50, $100

United Kingdom

One pound = 100 pence
Coins:
1p, 5p, 10p, 20p, 50p, £1, £2
(one "pee", five "pee", etc.)
Notes:
£5, £10, £20, £50

$1.25   one dollar twenty-five
$125   one hundred and twenty-five dollars
£1.25   one pound twenty-five
$2.39   two dollars thirty-nine cents
£2.39   two pounds thirty-nine
$1.50 / £1.50   one dollar fifty, one pound fifty (NOT ~~one and a half dollars / pounds~~)

Note: In the U.S. and Canada, amounts of paper money are called bills, in the U.K., notes.

VOCABULARY FILE 6: *colors*

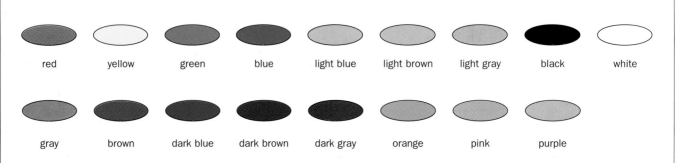

red   yellow   green   blue   light blue   light brown   light gray   black   white

gray   brown   dark blue   dark brown   dark gray   orange   pink   purple

VOCABULARY FILE 7: *time*

The 24-hour clock is not often used in the U.S.A. Use:
1 a.m. (01:00) / 1 p.m. (13:00)
3 a.m. (03:00) / 9 p.m. (21:00)

It is used for the military and ships:
01:00 "oh" one hundred hours
05:00 "oh" five hundred hours

In Britain, the 24-hour clock is used by airlines, railways,
and other timetables.
(You can also use a.m. / p.m. in conversation)

Timetables / appointments:

12:00 – twelve
12:10 – twelve ten
12:15 – twelve fifteen
12:30 – twelve thirty
12:45 – twelve forty-five
12:57 – twelve fifty-seven

Conversation:

12:00   twelve o'clock
12:05   twelve "oh" five / five after twelve (U.S.) / five past twelve (U.K.)
12:04   "oh" four / four minutes after / past twelve
12:57   three minutes to one / twelve fifty-seven
12:10   twelve ten / ten after / past twelve
12:15   twelve fifteen / (a) quarter after / past twelve
12:20   twelve twenty / twenty after / past twelve

12:25   twelve twenty-five / twenty-five after / past twelve
12:30   twelve thirty / half past twelve
12:35   twelve thirty-five / twenty five to one
12:40   twelve forty / twenty to one
12:45   twelve forty-five / (a) quarter to one
12:50   twelve fifty / ten to one
12:55   twelve fifty-five / five to one
01:00   one o'clock

Communication Activities

A

Unit 3 Landing Card – Student 1

LANDING CARD
Immigration Act 1971

Please complete clearly in BLOCK CAPITALS Por favor completar claramente en MAYUSCULAS
Veuillez remplir lisiblement en LETTRES MAJUSCULES Bitte deutlich in DRUCKSCHRIFT ausfüllen

Family name
Nom de famille
Apellidos
Familienname
Forenames
Prenoms
Nombre(s) de Pila
Vornamen

Sex
Sexe
Sexo (M,F)
Geschlecht

Date of birth Day Month Year
Date de naissance
Fecha de nacimiento
Geburtsdatum

Place of birth
Lieu de naissance
Lugar de nacimiento
Geburtsort

Nationality
Nationalite
Nacionalidad
Staatsangehörigkeit

Occupation
Profession
Profesion
Beruf

Address in United Kingdom
Adresse en Royaume Uni
Direccion en el Reino Unido
Adresse im Vereinigten Königreich

Signature
Firma
Unterschrift

EN 615 970

For official use /Reserve usage officiel/Para uso oficial/Nur für den Dienstgebrauch

CAT   -16   CODE   NAT   POL

1 You are an Immigration Officer in Britain. Student 2 is a visitor. Ask questions and complete the landing card with your partner's information, e.g.

What's your family name?
What's your middle initial?
What's your occupation / job?
What's your address on arrival in U.K.?

2 You are a visitor to Canada. Student 2 is a Canadian Immigration Officer. Help Student 2 fill out the Canadian Landing Card by answering their questions.

B

Unit 18 Itineraries – Student 1

1 You are a travel agent. Answer Student 2's questions about the Alaska tour.

2 Your partner is a travel agent. You are asking about a seven-night cruise to the Pacific Northwest.

SEVEN NIGHTS ALASKA TOUR
Vancouver – Skagway – Vancouver

date	day	cruise	arrive / depart
6/3	Sunday	Vancouver, B.C.	Board from 4 p.m.
6/4	Monday	Cruising the inside passage	
6/5	Tuesday	At sea viewing glaciers	
6/6	Wednesday	Skagway, Alaska Haines, Alaska	8 a.m. / 3 p.m. 6 p.m. / 10:30 p.m.
6/7	Thursday	Juneau, Alaska	7 a.m. / 6 p.m.
6/8	Friday	Ketchikan, Alaska Cruising Misty Fjord	8 a.m. / 3 p.m.
6/9	Saturday	At sea	
6/10	Sunday	Vancouver, B.C.	Arrive 10 a.m.

C

Unit 26 Routines – Student 1

First Student 2 is going to ask you about this daily routine:

THE PACIFIC RIM VOYAGER

Worksheet: Ken Nakamura, sports manager

7 a.m   Meet with sports organizers.
8 a.m. Open swimming pool.
9 a.m. Check passenger reservations for sports activities.
1 p.m. Lunch
2 p.m. Help with sports activities.
7 p.m. Dinner
8 p.m. Close swimming pool.
9 p.m. Take reservations for the next day.

Then you ask Student 2 about the daily routine they have. Find a time when Ken and Laura can meet.

Communication Activities

Unit 30 Arrangements – Student 1

You are going to do two role plays. In the first, you are a traveler in Vancouver. Student 2 is a travel agent. You want to get to St. Louis on Thursday night. Ask for information.

In the second, you are the travel agent. Student 2 is asking you about flights to San Diego. You have this information.

TO SAN DIEGO: THURSDAY

**Direct flight: American Airlines, 10:30
No other direct flights**

**Evening:
Air Canada to Los Angeles
DEPART: Vancouver 18:30
ARRIVE: Los Angeles International 20:45**

**Transfer to:
SkyWest to San Diego
DEPART: Los Angeles International 21:30
ARRIVE: San Diego 22:15**

Unit 33 About Yourself – Student 1

1 Student 2 is going to ask you about Edgar Young. You have this information about him:

	Edgar Young
Born:	Tampa, Florida
Education:	Master's degree in Business Administration
Work history:	Assistant manager – Delta Airlines, 3 years (in Atlanta)
	Travel agency manager – Chicago, 5 years
	Representative – AmCan Travel, Chicago, 2 years
	Manager, AmCan Travel, Seattle office, 6 years
	Now Sales Director, AmCan Travel, Vancouver

2 Student 2 has information about Alicia Romero. Ask questions about her.

Unit 36 Punctuation – Student 1

Dictate the letter below to Student 2. Dictate all the punctuation.

August 25
Apple Travel
Hollywood Boulevard
Los Angeles, California

Dear Ms. Smith,

Thank you for your telephone message. I was in New York.
I enclose these videotapes:

A Cruise to Alaska
Enjoy your vacation!
On board the "Pacific Rim Traveler"
A guide to Vancouver / Vancouver Island

Please call me (on extension 217) if you want more copies.
Sincerely,

(your name)

Unit 47 Sales Talk – Student 1

First you are a sales representative. Tell Student 2 about this product:

**AMAZING ALASKA
SUNTAN LOTION**
– Made in Alaska!

Amazing Alaska is sold in one liter bottles,
and costs $2.95 a bottle.
It's the cheapest suntan lotion.
Alaska is the coldest state in the U.S.A.
But the sun is very bright in the summer.
Sunburn is very dangerous.
Amazing Alaska stops sunburn.
Oil is produced in Alaska.
Amazing Alaska is made from oil.

Then listen to Student 2. They're going to try to sell you a product.

Communication Activities

Unit 52 Checking Out – Student 1

You are the manager of the Quantity Inn hotel in San Diego. There are two "Guests Comments" forms in every room. Mr. Edgar Young checked out last week, and he gave the reception clerk a blank Guest Comments form – he completed one, but took it with him by mistake. You have a blank form. You are calling Mr. Young and asking about his stay.

Quantity Inn
San Diego
GUEST COMMENTS

Please take a few minutes to complete this form.
You may leave it with reception or mail it to us.

	Excellent	Good	Fair	Poor
RECEPTION Was your check-in fast? Was your check-out fast? Were our reception clerks friendly?				
YOUR BEDROOM Was your room clean? Was it comfortable? Did you like the furniture?				
TELEPHONE SERVICE Were our operators friendly and polite? Was the service fast?				
ROOM SERVICE Was the service fast? Did you like our menu? Was the food good?				
QUANTITY RESTAURANT What did you think of the quality of food? What was the service like? Did you like our menu?				
HOUSEKEEPING What was our laundry service like? Did the room maid clean your room well?				

EMPLOYEES
Do any of our staff deserve special thanks?

....

AND FINALLY …
Was this your first stay at a Quantity Inn?
Would you like to stay with us again?

PERSONAL DETAILS:
Name: .... Room no: .... Dates of stay: ....

Thank you for helping us.

Miranda Hapsburg, General Manager,
Quantity Inn Hotels Group, Cleveland, Ohio

Unit 57 Skagway – Student 1

Role-play passengers asking for more information about the excursions. You have information about Excursion 6/01. Student 2 has information about excursion 6/02.

1 You are the tour guide. Student 2 is going to ask you about the excursion.

PACIFIC RIM VOYAGER
Thursday June 6th, Skagway Excursions
Fact sheet

EXCURSION 6/01
Railroad Ride White Pass & Yukon Railroad

Starting time:	8:30
Leaves from:	Railroad depot on Broadway & 2nd Avenue Depot is walking distance from the cruise ship.
Length of excursion:	5 hours (return 1:30 p.m.)
Cost per person:	$52.00
Stopping points:	White Pass Summit; Fraser, British Columbia (no visas required)

2 You are a passenger. You want to ask about excursion 6/02. You want this information:

When does it leave?
Where does it leave from?
There are five in my party. Can we travel together?
How much is it? Are the kids half price?
Do we need special clothes?
How long will we be on the glacier?
Is it dangerous?

Communication Activities

Unit 7 Arriving at a Hotel – Student 1

Interview another student, and complete the registration card with his/her details.

COLUMBIA TOWERS HOTEL,
Vancouver, B.C.

Guest Registration Card

Room number: ☐☐☐☐
Family name: ☐☐☐☐☐☐☐☐☐☐
First name(s): ☐☐☐☐☐☐☐☐☐☐
Home address:
Street: ☐☐☐☐☐☐☐☐☐☐☐
City: ☐☐☐☐☐☐☐☐☐☐
Zip code: ☐☐☐☐☐☐
Nationality: ☐☐☐☐☐☐☐☐☐☐
Passport number: ☐☐☐☐☐☐☐☐
Company name: ☐☐☐☐☐☐☐☐☐☐☐
Company address: ☐☐☐☐☐☐☐☐☐☐
☐☐☐☐☐☐☐☐☐☐
Car license number: ☐☐☐☐☐☐☐
Date of arrival: ☐☐☐☐☐☐
Date of departure: ☐☐☐☐☐☐
Method of payment: ☐☐☐☐☐☐☐☐☐

☐ On account ☐ American Express
☐ MasterCard ☐ Diner's Club
☐ Visa ☐ By check ☐ Cash

Signature: _____
Date: ☐☐☐☐☐☐

Unit 60 Good-Bye – Student 1

Happy Ending: One year later.
After the cruise, Josie and Ken telephoned each other every day. In September, Josie moved to the *Pacific Rim Explorer*. Josie and Ken were married in March. Cecilia Grant was Josie's Matron of Honor.
Alicia returned to San Diego. Simon Chang went there on vacation in December. Simon and Alicia are good friends. Alicia's brochure won a prize for "Best Advertising Pictures of The Year". Alicia now works for

herself. Her most recent series of pictures, *Movie Stars of The Year*, is a best-selling book.
Absolutely Arizona Mineral Waters was very popular. It's now the number three selling mineral water in North America. Now Jack can afford to stay at the best hotels, even at the Columbia Towers in Vancouver, where Pearl Li is now General Manager. Edgar Young lost his job at AmCan Travel. He's now a tour guide. He shows American tourists around England.

Student 2 has an unhappy ending. Discuss both endings, and decide on the most appropriate.

Unit 36 Punctuation – Student 2

Dictate the letter below to Student 1. Dictate all the punctuation.

January 30
Orange Travel
International Drive
Orlando, Florida

Dear Mr. Green,

Thank you for your fax. I was out of the office yesterday. I enclose the information brochures you need:

30 Air Canada timetables
100 Guide books to Vancouver
50 "I love Vancouver" stickers
10 San Diego / Los Angeles brochures

Please fax me (at the above number) if you want extra copies.

Sincerely yours,

(your name)

Communication Activities

Unit 6 A Ride Downtown – Student 2

Explain these words to your partner:

shuttle bus – a bus that leaves at regular times, and goes between two locations.

major downtown hotels – the big, important hotels in the center of the city.

every 30 minutes – e.g. the buses leave at 9:00, 9:30, 10:00, 10:30, etc.

meter – taxi cabs have a meter. The meter shows the cost – e.g. $1.20 per kilometer.

heavy traffic – at some times of day, there are a lot of cars, buses, motorcycles, and trucks (traffic). The traffic is heavy.

party – a group of people who are traveling together.

limousine – a large luxury vehicle (a car or a van). A limousine doesn't have a meter.

flat rate – the price is always the same. It's "fixed". There are no extras

transfer – to change from one bus or plane to a different bus or plane.

Unit 30 Arrangements – Student 2

You are going to do two role plays. In the first, you are a travel agent in Vancouver. Student 1 wants to get to St. Louis on Thursday night. They are leaving from Vancouver. You have this information:

ST. LOUIS: THURSDAY

Direct flight: Delta, 14:15
No other direct flights

Evening:
Continental to Chicago
DEPART: Vancouver 16:15 Pacific time
ARRIVE: Chicago 21:00 Central time
(Chicago is 2 hours in front of Vancouver.)

Transfer to:
Continental to St. Louis
DEPART: Chicago 21:40
ARRIVE: St. Louis 23:25

In the second, you are the traveler. Student 1 is the travel agent. You want to get to San Diego on Thursday night.

Unit 26 Routines – Student 2

First you ask Student 1 about the daily routine they have.

Then Student 1 is going to ask you about this daily routine:

THE PACIFIC RIM VOYAGER

Worksheet: Laura Patterson, Health Club Manager

7 a.m	Meet with Health Club personnel.
8 a.m.	Open club.
9 a.m.	Check passenger reservations for massages, trainers, saunas, etc.
11 a.m.	Take aerobics class.
1 p.m.	Lunch
2 p.m.	Work on Health Club reception desk.
5 p.m.	Take aerobics class.
6 p.m.	Dinner
9 p.m.	Close Health Club.

Find a time when Laura and Ken can meet.

Unit 18 Itineraries – Student 2

1 **Your partner is a travel agent. You are asking about a seven-night cruise to Alaska.**

2 **You are a travel agent. Answer Student 1's questions about the Pacific Northwest tour.**

SEVEN NIGHTS PACIFIC NORTHWEST CRUISE
Vancouver – Skagway – Vancouver

date	day	cruise	arrive / depart
6/10	Sunday	Vancouver, B.C.	Board from 4 p.m.
6/11	Monday	Alert Bay, B.C.	9 a.m. / 1 p.m.
6/12	Tuesday	Victoria, B.C.	8 a.m. / 6 p.m.
6/13	Wednesday	Seattle, Washington	8 a.m. / 5:30 p.m.
6/14	Thursday	Cruising Puget Sound Tacoma, Washington	4 p.m. / 9 p.m.
6/15	Friday	Eureka, California	1 p.m. / 6 p.m.
6/16	Saturday	Cruising the Pacific	
6/17	Sunday	Vancouver, B.C.	Arrive 11 a.m.

Communication Activities

Unit 47 Sales Talk – Student 2

First listen to Student 1. They're going to try to sell you a product.

Then, you are a sales representative. Tell Student 1 about this product:

PITTSBURG GENUINE
Italian Pizza

The cheese is produced in Wisconsin.

But the recipe is from Parma in Italy.

Perfect Pizza is deep-frozen.

Pittsburg Pizzas are the most expensive in your supermarket.

It's made in Pittsburg, Pennsylvania.

The basil is produced in Pennyslvania.

The tomatoes are produced in Florida.

They cost $15.99 each.

BUT THEY'RE THE BEST.

Unit 57 Skagway – Student 2

Role-play passengers asking for more information about the excursions. You have information about Excursion 6/02. Student 1 has information about excursion 6/01.

1 You are a passenger. You want to ask about excursion 6/01. You want this information:

When does the train leave?
Where does it leave from?
How do you get there?
The ship is in Skagway from 8 a.m. to 3 p.m. Will there be time to look around Skagway?
How much is it?

2 You are the tour guide. Student 1 is going to ask you about the excursion.

PACIFIC RIM VOYAGER

Thursday June 6th, Skagway Excursions
Fact sheet

EXCURSION 6/02
Glacier Flightseeing

Starting times:	8:30 then every half hour until 1:30 Heliport is walking distance from the ship. Note: Each flight takes six passengers only. There are TWO helicopters.
Total excursion time:	about one hour
Cost per person:	$130 – no child fares All equipment – boots and ski suit – is supplied.
Flight time:	about 15 minutes each way
Time on the glacier:	about 20 minutes
	There is a guide.

Unit 49 Let's Make a Deal – Student 2

Ask questions and complete the table.

	Albion-America	Pacific Rim Cruises
number of ships	7	
average age of ships	20 years	
average number of cabins per ship	850	
passengers last year	238,000	
cabins with balconies	60 on each ship	
restaurants per ship	two	
cinemas per ship	none	
video channels on TV	three	
swimming pools per ship	two	
average vacation cost for 7 days	$2,750	

Communication Activities

Unit 52 Checking Out – Student 2

You are going to role-play Edgar Young. There are two "Guests Comments" forms in every room at the Quantity Inn hotel in San Diego. You checked out last week, and you gave the reception clerk a blank Guest Comments form – you completed one, but took it with you by mistake. You have the completed form. The hotel manager is calling you and asking about your stay. Answer using your completed form.

Quantity Inn
San Diego
GUEST COMMENTS

Please take a few minutes to complete this form.
You may leave it with reception or mail it to us.

	Excellent	Good	Fair	Poor
RECEPTION				
Was your check-in fast?		✔		
Was your check-out fast?			✔	
Were our reception clerks friendly?				✔
YOUR BEDROOM				
Was your room clean?	✔			
Was it comfortable?		✔		
Did you like the furniture?				✔
TELEPHONE SERVICE				
Were our operators friendly and polite?				✔
Was the service fast?				✔
ROOM SERVICE				
Was the service fast?				✔
Did you like our menu?				✔
Was the food good?				✔
QUANTITY RESTAURANT				
What did you think of the quality of food?		✔		
What was the service like?				✔
Did you like our menu?			✔	
HOUSEKEEPING				
What was our laundry service like?		✔		
Did the room maid clean your room well?				✔

EMPLOYEES
Do any of our staff deserve special thanks?   *No! I complained to you, and you were very rude. You didn't listen to me.*

AND FINALLY …
Was this your first stay at a Quantity Inn?   *Unfortunately, no.*
Would you like to stay with us again?   *Certainly not.*

PERSONAL DETAILS:
Name: *E. Young*   Room no: *213*   Dates of stay: *May 23rd to June 1st*

Thank you for helping us.

Miranda Hapsburg, General Manager,
Quantity Inn Hotels Group, Cleveland, Ohio

Unit 60 Good-Bye – Student 2

Unhappy Ending: One year later.
After the cruise, Josie and Ken never saw each other again. Ken was only interested in his job. Josie was tired of cruise ships, and she returned to Britain. Alicia returned to San Diego. AmCan Travel bought Sagebrush Tours in November. Edgar Young became the Chief Executive Officer and moved to San Diego. Alicia had several arguments with him. She left the new company (AmCan-Sagebrush) in January. She now takes pictures of tourists in Las Vegas for $1.95 a picture. She never saw Simon Chang again. Simon left Pacific Rim Cruises in April, at the same time as the Columbia Towers Hotel fired Pearl Li because she was rude to an important customer (Edgar Young). Simon now works for AmCan Travel. He hates Edgar Young. Jack Hudson doesn't work for Absolutely Arizona anymore. After the salmonella outbreak on the *Pacific Rim Voyager* in August, Absolutely Arizona went bust. Jack is unemployed.

Student 1 has a happy ending. Discuss both endings, and decide on the most appropriate.

Unit 58 Souvenirs – Shop Assistant

Here is some information about the items on sale. Read it before you bargain with the customer!
A wooden carving of a bear:
Retail price: $195 / Cost: $100
Shipping (U.S./Canada) approximately $12.50 each

Pure wool blankets:
Retail price: $95 / Cost: $70 (they're on sale because you have a lot of them.)
Shipping (U.S./Canada) about $20 each (they're heavy!)

Cotton T-shirts:
Retail: $16.95 / Cost: $11.95
Shipping about $3.25

Chocolates:
Retail: $5.99 / Cost: $3.50
Shipping about $3.25 each

Photographs in frames:
Retail: $19.99 / Cost: pictures 75¢, frame $3.99 (you put them together in the shop.)
Shipping $6 (there is glass in the frames.)

Communication Activities

Unit 7 Arriving at a Hotel – Student 2

Interview another student, and complete the registration card with his/her details.

Quantity Inn
San Diego

REGISTRATION

Room:

Title/Military rank:
(Mr./Mrs./Ms./Other):

Family name:

First name:

Middle initial:

Address:

Street:

City:

Zip:

Home telephone:

Business name:

Business address:

Business telephone:

Business fax:

Car license plate:

Arrived:

Departed:

Payment by:

☐ Visa ☐ American Express
☐ MasterCard ☐ Quantity Inn Card
☐ Other

Signature: _____

Date (Month /Day/Year):

Unit 3 Landing Card – Student 2

CREW   IMM.   F.R.

We will use your answers to the following questions for customs control purposes, and to compile statistical data.

All travellers must complete this section

Last name | First name and initials | Date of birth (D M Y)

Address — Number, street | Postal code

City, town | Province or state | Country

Arriving by:
☐ Air — Name of airline — Flight no. | ☐ Marine | ☐ Rail | ☐ Other

Arriving from (check one):
☐ U.S. only (including Hawaii)
☐ Other country direct
☐ Other country via the U.S.

List the last 3 countries you visited on this trip (other than the U.S.):

Primary purpose of travel: ☐ Personal ☐ Business

I am bringing into Canada: Yes No
- goods that exceed my personal exemption limits or gift entitlement **(see information sheet)**; ☐ ☐
- goods such as firearms or other weapons, or articles made or derived from endangered species; ☐ ☐
- business material, professional goods, commercial goods, goods for resale, samples, tools, equipment; ☐ ☐
- animals, birds, meats, any food containing meat, dairy products, eggs; ☐ ☐
- plants, cuttings, grapevines, vegetables, fruits, seeds, nuts, bulbs, roots, soil. ☐ ☐

I will be visiting a farm in Canada within the next 14 days. ☐ ☐

All residents of Canada must complete this section

I left Canada on (D M Y). The total value of all goods I purchased, received, or acquired abroad, and goods I purchased at duty-free shops, for importation into Canada is: $ ___ Value in Canadian funds

The above amount includes unaccompanied goods valued at: $ ___ Value in Canadian funds

I qualify for and hereby claim a personal exemption of:
☐ CAN$50 ☐ CAN$200 ☐ CAN$500

E311 (95/05)   Signature of traveller   *444*

1 **You are a visitor to Britain. Student 1 is a British Immigration Officer. Help Student 1 fill out the British landing card by answering their questions.**

2 **You are an Immigration Officer in Canada. Student 1 is a visitor. Ask questions and complete the landing card with your partner's information, e.g.**

What's your first name?
What's your date of birth / address
Where are you arriving from?
What's the purpose of your visit?

Communication Activities

Y

Unit 33 About Yourself – Student 2

1 Student 1 has information about Edgar Young. Ask questions about him.

2 Student 1 is going to ask you about Alicia Romero. You have this information about her:

ALICIA ROMERO

Born:	*San Diego, California*
School:	*San Diego*
College:	*USC (University of Southern California), San Diego, 4 years*
	Degree in Art (majoring in Photography)
Experience:	*Photographic assistant: Kiddie Portraits, Del Mar, 4 weeks*
	Photographic assistant, San Diego Sun newspaper, 2 years
	Official photographer, Janet Jackson U.S. Tour, 3 months.
	Now: Photographer, Sagebrush Tours

Z

Unit 25 Picking Up a Car – Both Students

Complete the Express Car Rental form.

EXPRESS CAR RENTALS

Driver's name: _____
Other drivers (names): _____
Drivers license #: _____
Address: _____
Street: _____
City: _____
Zip: _____
Tel: _____
Fax: _____

Credit card #:

☐ MasterCard ☐ Visa ☐ Amex ☐ Diner's Club

☐☐☐☐ ☐☐☐☐ ☐☐☐☐☐

Expiration date: _____

Collision Damage Waiver (initial here) _____
Personal Accident Insurance (initial here) _____

CAR:
MAKE _____ MODEL _____
LICENSE # _____ DAILY RATE _____
Signature: _____

Transcripts

1 Numbers

EXERCISE 2

Check-in Clerk: There's your boarding pass, Mrs. Castellano. Flight AA 251 to Boston. Seat 15E. It departs from Gate 9 at 18:30.

EXERCISE 3

Voice: Good evening. Cross Globe Airways flight CG 185 to Vancouver is now ready for boarding. We are boarding the airplane in sections. Please have your boarding passes on hand. Passengers with small children and passengers with difficulties can board the airplane now … next, all those passengers in rows 39 through 56 … next, all those passengers between rows 20 and 38 … next, Business Class passengers seated in rows 6 through 19. Finally, First Class passengers in rows one through five.

3 Landing Card

EXERCISE 1

Video recording: This is your I-94 Arrival Record. Please complete it in ink and in block capitals. Section 1: write your family name – don't forget the block capitals. Section 2 is for your first or "given" name. In section 3, write your birth date. First the day, then the month, and finally the year. Section 4 is for your country of citizenship. Section 5 is sex – male or female. In section 6, put your passport number, then in 7, your airline and flight number. This is on your boarding pass, for example British Airways Flight 177 – write BA 177. For American Airlines Flight 210, write AA 210. In 8, write the country where you are living now, and in section 9, the city where you boarded this flight. For section 10, look at your visa in your passport. Write the city where the visa was issued, and in section 11 the date of your visa. Again, write day, then month, then year. Section 12 is your first address in the United States – put the number and street here. In section 13, write the city and the state. Put your I-94 in your passport, and hand it to Immigration control in the United States. Thank you for listening.

7 Arriving at a Hotel

EXERCISE 1

Edgar: Does it have a king-size bed?
Reception Clerk: Uh, no. No, it doesn't. It has a single bed.
Edgar: And does it have a bath?
Reception Clerk: A bath? No, it doesn't. But it has a shower. A small shower.
Edgar: I guess it has a TV.
Reception Clerk: Oh, yes. All our rooms have TVs. It has a small TV.
Edgar: Do you have in-room movies?
Reception Clerk: Yes sir. We have six channels of movies.
Edgar: And a room safe. Does it have a room safe?
Reception Clerk: No, it doesn't. But you can leave your valuables here at reception. You can put them in a safety deposit box.
Edgar: I need a drink. Does it have a mini-bar?
Reception Clerk: Uh, no. No mini-bar. You can buy drinks from vending machines in the hallway. There's an ice machine in the hallway too. It's right outside your room. You have the ice machine on one side of your room and the elevator on the other. It's very convenient.

Edgar: And the kitchen is under my room?
Reception Clerk: That's right. And the video games arcade is right across the hall!
Edgar: It's not a quiet room then.
Reception Clerk: Quiet? No, it's not quiet. But it's the only room we have.
Edgar: OK. I'll take it.
Reception Clerk: OK. Room 213. Can you just complete this registration card for me?

10 Breakfast Buffet

EXERCISE 1

Edgar: (Ouch! That's hot … where's a fork? Ow! That's hot too. Ah, yes. Sausages … one, two sausages … two fried eggs, and hash browns. Yes. A lot of hash browns. Any French toast? Oh, yes. There it is. Two … no, three, four pieces of French toast, it's the same price. There isn't any bacon!)
Excuse me, do you have any bacon?
Server: Bacon? No, sorry. There is't any left.
Edgar: OK. (Mm, some scrambled eggs and ham, then. Forget the cholesterol!)

EXERCISE 2

Edgar: Excuse me, is there any maple syrup for the French toast?
Server: Sure. It's right there in front of you.
Edgar: OK … (Hmm. A lot of maple syrup. Ooh, that's too much! Oh, it's OK. Actually, I'll just take it with me. Some milk for my coffee, that's great. Hmm. Breakfast rolls or English muffins? I don't know. Aw, an English muffin with jam. That's fine.)
Excuse me, is there any salt and pepper?
Server: There you go.
Edgar: OK thanks. (Is this enough food? I can always go back later …)

13 Concierge Desk

EXERCISE 1

Conversation 1:

Peter: Good morning, sir. Can I help you?
Man: Yes. I want to get a ticket for the concert at the Queen Elizabeth Theatre tonight.
Peter: The Montreal Symphony?
Man: That's right. Do you think it's possible?
Peter: I can call TicketMaster for you. How many do you want?
Man: Just the one.
Peter: Just a moment … Hello. This is the concierge at the Columbia Towers. Do you have a ticket for the Montreal Symphony? OK … can you hold it for me? Thanks. Yes, that's OK, sir. I can send a bellman, or you can collect it at Ticketmaster.
Man: I can collect it. Where's TicketMaster?
Peter: They have a booth in the Pacific Centre Mall. It's right across the street. Go out of the hotel, walk past the Stock Exchange, and take a left into the mall. Go up one level. TicketMaster's on that level. You can follow the signs.

Conversation 2:

Peter: Good morning, sir, madam. Can I help you?
Woman: Please. We're going to the Marine Building. Can you direct us?
Peter: Sure. It's about a ten-minute walk. Go out the hotel entrance, and turn right onto Dunsmuir

Street. Go left along Dunsmuir for three blocks. At Burrard take a right, and walk a couple of blocks toward the waterfront. The Marine Building's on the left hand side … here. You can take the map with you.
Woman: Thank you.

Conversation 3:

Woman: Excuse me!
Peter: Yes, ma'am.
Woman: I'm looking for a good souvenir shop.
Peter: The hotel shop has souvenirs; it's right over there.
Woman: It's too expensive!
Peter: Well, there are souvenir shops in the Pacific Centre and on Robson Street, or you can go to Gastown. There are a lot of good souvenir shops down there. I recommend Gastown. It's the old part of the city.
Woman: OK. How do I get there?
Peter: Well, it's a ten to fifteen-minute walk … You can …
Woman: Fifteen minutes! No way. Where can I take a cab?
Peter: You can find one right outside the hotel entrance.
Woman: Thanks.

20 Connections

EXERCISE 2

Call 1, part 1:

Edgar: Try again … 9-321-7844.
Message: Thank you for calling Sagebrush Tours …
Edgar: Good morning …
Message: …Your call is in a call-waiting system. Please hold until one of our telephone operators is free …
Edgar: Come on!
Message: Thank you for holding. Your call is still in a call-waiting system. Please hold until one of our telephone operators is free …
Edgar: Oh, no, I don't have all day!
Message: Thank you for holding. Your call is …
Edgar: Finally!
Operator: Pardon me?

EXERCISE 3

Call 1, part 2:

Operator: Sagebrush Tours. Thank you for waiting. This is Michael speaking. How may I help you?
Edgar: May I speak to Ms. Lowe, please?
Operator: Please hold. I'm connecting you.
Edgar: Thank you.

EXERCISE 4

Call 1, part 3:

Answering machine: Hello, this is Cathy Lowe. I'm not at my desk right now. Please leave your name and number after the tone, and I'll call you back. Thank you for calling.
Edgar: Ah, yes. Right. Good morning, Ms. Lowe. How are you? I'm in San Diego for a few days, for business, and I want to meet with you about your travel brochure for next year. Right now I'm staying at the Quantity Inn downtown, near Balboa Park, and I … Oh, no! That's the end of the message. My name! She doesn't have my name! OK, I can call again this afternoon …

EXERCISE 6

Call 2:

Edgar: Right. 9, then 715-0921.

Message: This is Sunburst Travel. If you are calling from a touch-tone phone, press 5 for reservations; press 3 for recorded information; press 7 if you want a brochure. For other inquiries press 0, or hold the line for an operator.

Edgar: Is this a touch-tone phone? I guess so, press 0.

Operator: Sunburst Travel. Can I help you?

Edgar: Right! Can I speak to Steve Cantor, please?

Operator: Mr. Cantor isn't in the office today. Do you want his assistant?

Edgar: No. I can call tomorrow. Thanks anyway.

Operator: You're welcome.

21 Fast Food

EXERCISE 2

Server: Hello again.

Jack: Hi. An ice cream, please.

Server: Would you like vanilla or chocolate or both?

Jack: Both.

Server: There you go. One eighty-one with the tax.

Jack: OK.

Server: Hmm. I can't make change for a fifty. Do you have anything smaller?

Jack: Oh, yeah. Here's a two-dollar bill.

Server: Thanks.

24 Car Rental Inquiries

EXERCISE 3

Call 1:

Clerk: Alumus Rent-A-Car. Downtown office. Can I help you?

Edgar: Yes, I want to rent a car for a few days … any size, any grade. It's not important.

Clerk: Do you have a pre-reservation, sir?

Edgar: No. Do I need one?

Clerk: We're pretty busy right now. Uh, when do you want it?

Edgar: Today. As soon as possible.

Clerk: I have some Economy grade vehicles. They're Dodge Colts. They're pretty small.

Edgar: Don't you have anything else?

Clerk: No, sir. I'm sorry.

Edgar: Hmm. Look, can I call you back later? I'd prefer a mid-size or a full-size.

Clerk: Sure. Thanks for calling.

Call 2:

Clerk: Express Car Rentals. Airport office. Melissa speaking. May I help you?

Edgar: Yes. I want to rent a car today. I need one as soon as possible. Do you have anything?

Clerk: Sure. What grade do you want?

Edgar: Full-size.

Clerk: Hmm. I don't have a full-size vehicle. But we have an offer on luxury cars this month. You can have a Cadillac Sedan de Ville for just $66 a day. Or I have a mid-size.

Edgar: $66 a day? What price do you have on mid-size?

Clerk: $48 a day.

Edgar: A mid-size, then. Can I pick it up here in San Diego and drop it off at L.A. International?

Clerk: Sure, but there's a fifty dollar drop-off charge.

Edgar: That's OK. I'm coming right over. Can you hold the car for me?

Clerk: Sure. What's your name?

Edgar: Young. Edgar Young.

Clerk: OK, Mr. Young. See you soon.

27 Structures

Alicia: So, Simon. What's your job here?

Simon: I'm Mr. Dawson's assistant.

Alicia: Who's Mr. Dawson?

Simon: He's the Publicity Manager. You're going to meet him this afternoon.

Alicia: Right. What do you do exactly?

Simon: I'm responsible for brochures – our own brochures and brochures from travel agencies – like Sagebrush Tours.

Alicia: So, Mr. Dawson's your boss?

Simon: Not exactly. He's just the Head of my Department. No, Mr. Dawson reports to the Marketing Director, Mr. Burgess. Mr. Burgess is in charge of marketing, publicity, and sales.

Alicia: Do you do any work on the ships?

Simon: No, not really. The company has two divisions, sales and operations. Each division has a Veep – sorry, a Vice-President. For example, Mr. Burgess reports to the Vice-President in charge of sales … Her name's Ms. Ivanov. All the ships' captains report to Mr. Perez, who's responsible for all operations.

Alicia: So, Ms. Ivanov's the big boss then!

Simon: Uh, yes … for me, she's the big boss. Of course she has a boss, too. That's Patricia Brooke, the Chief Executive Officer. And I guess above her there's Sven Hansson, the company President.

Alicia: Wow! It sounds complicated.

Simon: It is. Believe me, it is!

30 Arrangements

EXERCISE 3

Jack: OK, forget direct flights. Can I transfer through another airport?

Agent: Yes … you can go via Denver. That flight won't leave Vancouver until six fifty-five.

Jack: When's the last check-in for economy class?

Agent: Six o'clock will be OK.

Jack: When will I get to Denver?

Agent: Nine twenty Mountain Time. It's an hour in front of Vancouver.

Jack: Uh huh, and when will the Phoenix flight leave?

Agent: Five after ten. But don't worry, you'll make it.

Jack: So, what time will I get to Phoenix?

Agent: By the time you get to Phoenix, it'll be ten after midnight. Do you want to take that flight?

Jack: Sure. That's fine.

32 Traveling in a Group

EXERCISE 4

Cecilia OK, Laura, you take the next cab with the Captain and Philip. I'll take the last one with Daniel and Marilyn.

Laura: OK.

Cecilia Tell the driver it's the Panama Hat restaurant. Tell him it's on Orange Avenue.

Laura: Fine.

Cecilia You pay the fare. Don't forget the receipt!

EXERCISE 6

Britanny: Is it OK if I sit up front?

Driver: Sure.

Kenji: The Panama Hat Restaurant. It's on Orange Avenue. Do you know it?

Driver: Yeah, sure, I know it! My brother works there.

34 Getting Through

EXERCISE 2

Part 1:

Operator: Thank you for calling Pacific Rim Cruises. This is Stephanie speaking. How may I help you?

Edgar: I want to speak to Simon Chang, please.

Operator: And may I say who's calling?

Edgar: Yes. This is Edgar Young of AmCan Travel.

Operator: Thank you, Mr. Young. Please hold.

EXERCISE 3

Part 2:

Secretary: This is Simon Chang's phone.

Operator: There's a Mr. Young from AmCan Travel on the line.

Secretary: Simon's in a meeting. Hold on. Simon?

Simon: Yes?

Secretary: Edgar Young's on the line. Do you want to speak with him?

Simon: No! Tell him I'm in a meeting, and tell him that I'll call him later.

Secretary: Hello? Put him through on my extension.

Operator: OK.

EXERCISE 4

Part 3:

Operator: I'm putting you through now.

Edgar: Thank you.

Secretary: This is Mr. Chang's assistant. How may I help you?

Edgar: Can I speak to Simon, please?

Secretary: I'm afraid he's in a meeting, Mr. Young. Can I take a message?

Edgar: It's important. Can't you interrupt him?

Secretary: I'm afraid not, Mr. Young. Do you want him to call you back?

Edgar: I guess so.

Secretary: Does he have your number?

Edgar: Yes, he does. Thank you.

Edgar: Oh, no! He has my number in Vancouver. He doesn't know that I'm in San Diego!

Unit 35 Explaining

EXERCISE 1

Simon: You see, AmCan represents our competition.

Alicia: I don't know much about this, Simon.

Simon: Let me explain. There are several cruise lines on the Alaska route, but Albion-America are the biggest. AmCan advertises Albion-America is their brochures.

Alicia: So why does he want to talk with you?

Simon: Because AmCan wants to represent Pacific Rim Cruises as well. But we don't want to do business with them.

Alicia: Why not?

Simon: Two reasons. Because they'll ask for a very large commission, and because we don't want to be in the same brochures as our competitors.

Alicia: Sounds reasonable to me. Well, Pacific Rim will be the only cruise line in Sagebrush's next brochure.

36 Punctuation

EXERCISE 2

Part 1:

```
Hamptons Travel                    May 24th
South Hampton
Long Island, New York

Dear Sir or Madam,

Thank you for your letter. We enclose the
following items:

400    Alaska Cruise brochures
200    Pacific NorthWest / Seattle brochures
150    General brochures
50     "Pacific Rim Voyager" cabin plans

Please call me (on extension 42) if you want
additional brochures. Do you want copies of
our hotel guide to Vancouver? It's new this
week! We can arrange hotel accommodation,
and a Vancouver sightseeing tour, before
passengers board the ship.

Yours truly,
Simon Chang
Publicity Department
```

EXERCISE 3

Part 2:

date May twenty fourth
This is to Hamptons Travel, South Hampton, Long Island, New York
space, then new line
Dear Sir or Madam comma,
space, then new line
Thank you for your letter period. We enclose the following items colon:
space, then new line
400 Alaska Cruise brochures
new line
200 Pacific NorthWest slash Seattle brochures
new line
150 General capital G brochures
new line
50 open quotation marks "Pacific Rim Voyager" close quotation marks cabin plans
space, then new line
Please call me open parentheses (on extension 42) close parentheses if you want additional brochures period. Do you want copies of our hotel guide to Vancouver question mark? It's new this week exclamation point! We can arrange hotel accommodation comma, and a Vancouver sightseeing tour comma, before passengers board the ship period.
space, then new line
Yours truly comma,
Simon Chang
etcetera

39 Important Messages

EXERCISE 2

Message 1:

Clerk: Pioneer Hotel.
Woman: Can I speak to Mr Hudson, please?

Clerk: Please hold … He's not in his room right now.
Woman: Can you take a message?
Clerk: Sure. No problem.
Woman: Ask him to call Ms. Alvarez's secretary at the Columbia Towers Hotel. Do you want me to spell that?
Clerk: No, ma'am. I can spell "secretary".
Woman: I mean "Alvarez".
Clerk: Oh. OK.
Woman: A-L-V-A-R-E-Z
Clerk: Huh. I got it right!

Message 2:

Clerk: Pioneer Hotel.
Man: Can I leave a message for a Mr. Jack Hudson?
Clerk: Sure.
Man: Ask him to call All Canada Airlines, at 604-551-0973.
Clerk: Can you repeat the number?
Man: 604-551-0973.
Clerk: OK, I got it. Let me check, 604-551-0973.
Man: Yes. That's it.

Message 3:

Clerk: Pioneer Hotel.
Woman: May I speak with Mr. Hudson, please.
Clerk: Did you say "Hudson"?
Woman: That's right.
Clerk: He's out of the building right now. Do you want me to take a message?
Woman: No, it's … Yes. Take a message. This is Sandra Davidson. Can he call me back Wednesday night?
Clerk: Right. You want him to call you back Wednesday night.
Woman: You will give it to him as soon as he gets back to the hotel?
Clerk: Yeah, sure. I won't forget.

40 Telephone Services

EXERCISE 3

Call 1:

Jack: Pierre Duchamps … he lives in Vancouver, so it's a local area code. OK. Just 555-1212.
Operator: Directory assistance. Which city?
Jack: Vancouver.
Operator: What name?
Jack: Duchamps, P.
Operator: Address?
Jack: I don't know … It's over in North Vancouver somewhere.
Recording: The number you require is 411-9008.

Call 2:

Jack: I don't have Darlene's number either. Ah, well. Directory assistance again. Phoenix – that's 1, 602, then 555-1212.
Operator: Directory assistance. Which city?
Jack: Scottsdale.
Operator: What name?
Jack: Kennedy, Darlene. North Highland Drive.
Recording: The number you require is 732-1190.

41 Attractions

EXERCISE 2

Description 1:

Simon: This is pretty difficult to get a picture of. The postcards usually have views from the bottom of the canyon – the canyon is seventy meters deep. Or you can take people walking across from one end. That's easy.

Description 2:

Simon: Everyone takes the same shot of this. The clock in the middle. You need a lot of people in the shot, and you could take shots of pavement cafés or boutiques as well. This is where the city started.

Description 3:

Simon: We need to ride this anyway, on our way to Capilano and Grouse Mountain. Anyway, while we're on board we can get some great shots of the waterfront and of North Vancouver. I think it's a good picture on its own. You don't get these everywhere!

Description 4:

Simon: The views are fantastic on a sunny day. You're 1200 meters up at the top. There's a chairlift up there – in the winter they use it for the ski run, in summer it's just a sightseeing ride.

43 The Menu

EXERCISE 3

Waiter: Hi there. My name's Ivan, and I'm your waiter for today. Do you want more time to look at the menu? No? OK, now our chef this evening is Jean-Paul, and everything on the menu is really great. Maybe I can give you my personal recommendation? Is that OK, folks? Well, I love everything on the menu, but tonight the grilled tuna steak is fantastic. This is deep-sea Bluefin tuna from unpolluted Pacific Ocean waters. It's grilled with a little genuine Italian olive oil, fresh basil and garlic, then a fresh lemon sauce – when I say fresh, I mean the sauce and the lemons are fresh – the lemons were picked from the tree this morning – the sauce is drizzled over the tuna. That comes with a vegetable selection; we have zucchini, eggplant, and tomato this evening …

EXERCISE 4

Cecilia

Waiter: OK, ma'am. Are you ready to order?
Cecilia Sure. I'll have the melon with Parma ham, followed by the steak.
Waiter: How do you want the steak?
Cecilia Mm, well done.
Waiter: OK. What do you want with that?
Cecilia The salad.
Waiter: Do you want a dressing on that?
Cecilia Yes. Uh, oil and vinegar.
Waiter: And for dessert? Do you want to order now or later?
Cecilia Now. Uh … the strawberries, please.
Waiter: OK. Thank you.

Ken

Waiter: Are you ready to order, sir?
Ken: Thanks. I'd like the spinach and bacon salad … Does that have a dressing?
Waiter: Yes, it does. It has an extra-virgin olive oil dressing with lime, garlic, and fresh herbs.
Ken: That's fine. And, uh, I'd like the tuna. It sounds great. With baked potato.
Waiter: Thank you. Would you like to order dessert now?
Ken: No. I'll choose dessert later. Thank you.
Waiter: You're welcome.

Josie

Waiter: And for you, ma'am?
Josie: Mm, I'll try the tomato and mozzarella salad for starters, uh, then the stir-fried vegetables, please.
Waiter: That comes on its own. Is that OK?
Josie: Yes, that's fine. Oh, and I'd like a Key Lime pie, please. Thanks.
Waiter: OK.

47 Sales Talk

EXERCISE 4

Marsha: Excuse me Mr. Hudson … my phone. Yes? Marsha speaking?
Stefan: Hello, Marsha. This is Stefan from Cruise Supplies Company.
Marsha: Stefan! Hello. I was going to call you back.
Stefan: I know. But there's a problem with your order.
Marsha: A problem? What kind of a problem?
Stefan: We have the Perrier. But we don't have three thousand extra bottles of Evian. We're going to get some next week …
Marsha: Next week? I need them for the *Pacific Rim Voyager* on Sunday, June 3rd.
Stefan: We'll have them on Monday the 4th.
Marsha: Monday's too late! I need them on Sunday.
Stefan: I'm very sorry, Marsha. There's nothing I can do.
Marsha: OK, thanks for calling.
Stefan: OK. Bye … and sorry again.
Marsha: Uh, Mr. Hudson?
Jack: Yes?
Marsha: Do you have three thousand bottles of Absolutely Arizona here in Vancouver?

Unit 50 Gas Station

EXERCISE 1

Clerk: OK, sir. That was twenty-three fifty-two. Now, you gave me thirty dollars. Is that correct?
Edgar: I have a flight to catch. Hurry up.
Clerk: OK. Out of thirty, that's fifty-three, four, five, and a nickel makes sixty, and four dimes makes twenty-four dollars, and one, and five makes thirty dollars. Now, do you want a receipt?
Edgar: Yes.
Clerk: And we have vouchers. You can get a free coffee cup with fifty vouchers …
Edgar: I don't want the vouchers. Just give me the receipt.
Clerk: OK. There you go, sir. Have a nice day.

53 Your Cabin

EXERCISE 3

Maria: OK, here's the TV. And here's the remote control. You can get the on-board information service on channel 1. It has a guide to the ship and information about excursions. Channel 2 is video movies. That operates 24 hours a day. And channel 3 is entertainment … cartoons, sit-coms, that kind of thing. From 6 a.m. to 6 p.m. it's mainly kid's programs. Channels 4 through 7 are satellite channels. Channel 4 is CNN News, then 5 is the sports channel – baseball and athletics, you know what I mean. Then 6 is satellite entertainment, and 7 is new movies. You can get information on your charge account on channel 8 …
Alicia: That's OK. Pacific Rim Cruises are picking up my tab!
Maria: Really? That's great. Then Channel 9 has children's video games. You can access various games.
Alicia: I don't think that one's for me!
Maria: Yeah. I don't like video games either.

56 Computer Problems

EXERCISE 3

Voice: May we remind passengers that the use of laptop computers, portable phones, CD players, and other electronic equipment is strictly prohibited on this flight.
Attendant: Excuse me, sir. Did you hear the announcement?
Edgar: Pardon me?
Attendant: Did you hear the announcement? You can't use your computer.
Edgar: But I'm right in the middle of an important document …
Attendant: Sorry, sir. You'll have to turn it off.
Edgar: Oh, come on! It's not dangerous.
Attendant: It can interfere with the airplane's equipment, sir. You'll have to turn it off.
Edgar: What? I want to speak to the pilot!
Attendant: You can't sir. We're taxiing out for take-off.
Voice: Would the flight attendants now take their seats for take-off …
Attendant: Give it to me, sir. I'll return it when we get to Anchorage …
Edgar: OK. But I'm never going to fly Air Canada again.
Attendant: Oh, really, sir? That doesn't matter to us. This is Air Alaska.

59 Good News

EXERCISE 3

Ken: Mr. Perez? This is Ken Nakamura speaking.
Mr. Perez: Where were you?
Ken: Sorry, Mr. Perez, I was coaching some passengers.
Mr. Perez: Do you know Mr. O'Connell?
Ken: Yes, I know Paul O'Connell. He's the Entertainment Director on the *Pacific Rim Explorer*.
Mr. Perez: Well, he had a bad accident. He fell over on a glacier.
Ken: Oh, dear. I'm sorry to hear that. How is he?

Mr. Perez: He's coming out of the hospital next week.
Ken: Good, it's not serious then.
Mr. Perez: He broke his leg badly. He's going to be away from work for six months.
Ken: Oh, I see. Six months?
Mr. Perez: That's right. You're going to be in Vancouver on Sunday, aren't you?
Ken: Yes, we're going to be in Vancouver on Sunday.
Mr. Perez: Well, I want you to be the new Entertainment Director on the *Pacific Rim Explorer*.
Ken: Sorry, can you say that again?
Mr. Perez: I want you to be the new Entertainment Director on the *Pacific Rim Explorer*.
Ken: Well, thank you. Thank you very much.
Mr. Perez: So, you'll take the job?
Ken: Yes, sure, I'll take it.
Mr. Perez: Good. Very good.
Ken: Uh, who's going to tell Cecilia Grant?
Mr. Perez: I called her this morning.
Ken: Right. She knows already.
Mr. Perez: And Syreeta Martin will take your job as Sports Manager on the *Voyager*. Is that OK?
Ken: Yes, Syreeta will be great.
Mr. Perez: Can you tell her?
Ken: Yes, I'll tell her right now.
Mr. Perez: Good-bye, Mr. Nakamura.
Ken: Good-bye, sir.

60 Good-Bye

EXERCISE 2

Will Josie and Ken meet again?
Will Ken be successful in his new job?
Will Alicia ever return to Vancouver?
Will Alicia see Simon Chang before she flies back to San Diego?
Will Pacific Rim Cruises buy more Absolutely Arizona mineral water?
Will Jack Hudson ever return to Canada?
Why did Edgar Young fly up to Anchorage?
Will Edgar Young finally meet with Alicia?
Will Alicia take pictures for AmCan Travel?

Wordlist

ENGLISH	FRENCH	JAPANESE	GERMAN
accident 24, 25	accident	事故	Unfall
accommodation 36	logement	客室	Unterkunft
address (n) 3, 7, 25, 46, 60	adresse	住所	Adresse
administration 8, 17, 26	administration	事務総括	Verwaltung
adult 41, 53	adulte	大人	Erwachsene(r)
advertise 35	faire de la publicité	広告する	werben
agree 23, 34	être d'accord	合意する	zustimmen
airline 30, 51	compagnie aérienne	航空会社	Fluggesellschaft
airplane 1, 3, 29, 31, 37, 48	avion	航空機	Flugzeug
airport 1, 5, 6, 23, 24, 51	aéroport	空港	Flughafen
announcement 1	annonce	発表	Ankündigung
answer (v) 31	répondre	答える	antworten
apartment 58	appartement	アパート	Wohnung
appointment 1, 9, 47, 49	rendez-vous	予約、約束	Termin
area 53, 54	zone	地域	Gebiet
arrange 36	arranger	手配する	vorbereiten
arrive 7, 18, 26, 30	arriver	到着する	ankommen
assistant 19, 27	assistant	アシスタント	Assistent
attendant 1, 3	gardien	係員	Stewardess
bag 4, 5, 6, 51	sac	バッグ	Tasche
baggage 5, 6, 51	bagages	手荷物	Gepäck
beautiful 12, 23, 55, 58	joli	美しい	schön
bell captain [UK: head porter] 15	portier principal	ベルキャプテン	erster Gepäckträger
bill 29	note	請求書	Rechnung
block (n) 13	pâté de maisons	ブロック	Block
board (v) 36	embarquer	搭乗する	an Bord gehen
boarding card/pass 1, 51	carte d'embarquement	搭乗券	Bordkarte
book (n) 9, 42	livre	本	Buch
border (n) 12	frontière	国境	Grenze
borrow 3	emprunter	借りる	leihen
bridge (n) 41	passerelle	橋	Brücke
brochure 9, 19, 20, 35, 36, 48, 49, 53	brochure	パンフレット	Broschüre
building 8, 12, 41	bâtiment	建物	Gebäude
business 3, 8, 11, 23, 35, 44, 53	commerce	ビジネス	Geschäft
busy 23, 30, 34, 53, 59	occupé	混雑した	beschäftigt
button (n) 8, 14	touche	ボタン	Knopf
buy 46, 60	acheter	買う	kaufen
cab 6, 32	taxi	タクシー	Taxi
cabin 36, 49, 53, 58	cabine	キャビン	Kabine
car 7, 11, 20, 24, 50	voiture	車	Auto
card 3, 9,18, 47, 52	carte	カード	Karte
carpet (n) 55	moquette	カーペット	Teppich
carry 49	porter	運ぶ	tragen
case (n) 5	conteneur	ケース	Koffer
cashier 29, 52	caissier	レジ	Kassierer
catch (v) 29, 50	prendre	乗る	kriegen
center (n) 1, 12, 13, 23	centre	センター	Zentrum
channel (n) 49, 53	chaîne	チャンネル	Kanal
check (n/v) 7, 22, 25, 26, 30, 52	chèque (n), vérifier (v)	n=小切手、v=確認する	Scheck (n), sicherstellen (v)
check in/out 7, 30, 51; 16, 29, 52	enregistrement entrée/sortie	チェックイン・チェックアウト	einchecken/abreisen

PORTUGUESE	ITALIAN	SPANISH	ENGLISH
acidente	incidente	accidente	accident 24, 25
acomodação	alloggio	alojamiento	accommodation 36
endereço	indirizzo	dirección	address (n) 3, 7, 25, 46, 60
administração	amministrazione	administración	administration 8, 17, 26
adulto	adulto	adulto	adult 41, 53
anunciar	fare pubblicità	hacer publicidad	advertise 35
concordar	essere d'accordo	estar de acuerdo	agree 23, 34
linha-aérea	compagnia aerea	aerolínea	airline 30, 51
avião	aeroplano	avión	airplane 1, 3, 29, 31, 37, 48
aeroporto	aeroporto	aeropuerto	airport 1, 5, 6, 23, 24, 51
anúncio	annuncio	anuncio	announcement 1
responder	rispondere	responder	answer (v) 31
apartamento	appartamento	apartamento	apartment 58
hora marcada	appuntamento	cita	appointment 1, 9, 47, 49
área	area	zona	area 53, 54
arranjar	disporre	organizar	arrange 36
chegar	arrivare	llegar	arrive 7, 18, 26, 30
assistente	assistente	asistente	assistant 19, 27
aeromoça	addetto	acompañante	attendant 1, 3
bolsa	valigia	valija	bag 4, 5, 6, 51
bagagem	bagagli	equipaje	baggage 5, 6, 51
bonito	bello	hermoso	beautiful 12, 23, 55, 58
porteiro principal	portabagagli	conserje principal	bell captain [UK: head porter] 15
conta	conto	cuenta	bill 29
quarteirão	isolato	bloque de viviendas	block (n) 13
embarcar	imbarcarsi	embarcarse	board (v) 36
cartão de embarque	carta di imbarco	tarjeta de embarque	boarding card/pass 1, 51
livro	libro	libro	book (n) 9, 42
fronteira	confine, frontiera	frontera	border (n) 12
tomar emprestado	prendere a prestito	pedir prestado	borrow 3
ponte	ponte	puente	bridge (n) 41
folheto	opuscolo	folleto	brochure 9, 19, 20, 35, 36, 48, 49, 53
prédio	edificio	edificio	building 8, 12, 41
negócio	attività commerciale	negocio	business 3, 8, 11, 23, 35, 44, 53
ocupado	occupato	ocupado	busy 23, 30, 34, 53, 59
botão	pulsante	botón	button (n) 8, 14
comprar	acquistare	comprar	buy 46, 60
taxi	tassì	taxi	cab 6, 32
cabine	cabina	cabina	cabin 36, 49, 53, 58
carro	automobile	coche	car 7, 11, 20, 24, 50
cartão	scheda	tarjeta	card 3, 9,18, 47, 52
carpete	tappeto	alfombra	carpet (n) 55
carregar	portare	llevar	carry 49
mala	astuccio, contenitore	valija	case (n) 5
caixa	cassiere	cajero	cashier 29, 52
pegar	prendere	tomar	catch (v) 29, 50
centro	centro	centro	center (n) 1, 12, 13, 23
canal	canale	canal	channel (n) 49, 53
cheque (n), verificar (v)	assegno (n), verificare (v)	cheque (n), verificar (v)	check (n/v) 7, 22, 25, 26, 30, 52
registro de entrada / de saída	firmare il registro dell'albergo / lasciare libera la stanza	firmar el registro/pagar e irse	check in/out 7, 30, 51; 16, 29, 52

ENGLISH	FRENCH	JAPANESE	GERMAN
choice 28, 53	choix	選択	Wahl
citizen 3	citoyen	市民	Bürger
city 4, 7, 11, 12, 23, 41, 47, 54	cité	都市	Stadt
clerk (n) 33	réceptionniste	事務官	Angestellte(r)
climate 12	climat	気候	Klima
climb (n) 48	ascension	上昇	Aufstieg
close (v) 51, 53	fermer	閉める	schließen
coach (n) 33, (v) 59	entraîneur (n), entraîner (v)	n=コーチ、v=コーチする	Trainer (n), trainieren (v)
coast (n) 9, 12, 18	côte	海岸	Küste
cold 12, 19, 23, 29	froid	寒い	kalt
college 33	collège	カレッジ	Hochschule
command (n) 56	commande	命令	Befehl
commission (n) 35, 49	commission	手数料	Provision
company (n) 7, 28, 32, 34, 46	société	企業	Unternehmen
competition (n) 35, 45	concurrence	競争	Wettbewerb
computer 7, 17, 42, 45, 46, 56	ordinateur	コンピューター	Computer
concierge 11, 13	concierge	コンシェルジュ	Concierge
conference 8	conférence	会議	Konferenz
confirm 9	confirmer	確認	bestätigen
connect 20, 56	relier	接続	verbinden
contact (v) 25, 46, 60	contacter	連絡する	in Verbindung setzen
copy (n) 36, 52, 56	exemplaire	コピー	Kopie
country 12, 22, 47, 51	pays	国	Land
credit (n) 25, 40, 50	crédit	クレジット	Kredit
crew 55	équipage	クルー	Crew, Team
cruise (n/v) 16, 18, 19, 47, 49, 52, 53	croisière (n), faire une croisière (v)	巡航（する）	Kreuzfahrt (n), eine Kreuzfahrt machen (n)
daily 26	quotidiennement	毎日の（に）	täglich
dangerous 57	dangereux	危険	gefährlich
day 20, 24, 25, 26, 30, 50, 54	jour	日	Tag
decide 49	décider	決める	entscheiden
degree 33	licence	学位	Hochschulabschluß
deliver 46, 47	livrer	配達する	ausliefern
department 17, 27, 31, 34, 42	département	部門	Abteilung
departure 1, 3, 51	départ	出発	Abfahrt
desk 11, 13, 29, 53	bureau	デスク	Schreibtisch
dial (v) 34	composer	ダイヤルする	wählen
different 13, 21, 50	différent	違う	verschieden
direct (adj.) 30, 34	direct(e)	直接	direkt
director 16, 17, 27, 59	directeur	取締役	Direktor
disagree 34	être en désaccord	反対する	nicht übereinstimmen
disc 53, 56	disque	ディスク	Diskette
discount (n) 58	rabais	割引	Rabatt
discover 57	découvrir	発見する	entdecken
discuss 9	discuter	話し合う	diskutieren
disturb 15, 34, 42	déranger	邪魔する	stören
doctor (n) 16, 27, 31	docteur	医師	Arzt
document 56	document	書類	Unterlage
dollar 22, 24, 50	dollar	ドル	Dollar
door 6, 8, 17, 38, 47, 53	porte	ドア	Tür
drink (n/v) 2, 19, 28, 48, 56; 42, 55	boisson (n), boire (v)	飲み物・飲む	Getränk (n), trinken (v)

PORTUGUESE	ITALIAN	SPANISH	ENGLISH
escolha	scelta	elección	choice 28, 53
cidadão	cittadino	ciudadano	citizen 3
cidade	città	ciudad	city 4, 7, 11, 12, 23, 41, 47, 54
funcionário	impiegato	oficinista	clerk (n) 33
clima	clima	clima	climate 12
escalada	salita	subida	climb (n) 48
fechar	chiudere	cerrar	close (v) 51, 53
treinador (n), treinar (v)	allenatore (n), allenare (v)	entrenador (n), entrenar (v)	coach (n) 33, (v) 59
costa	costa	costa	coast (n) 9, 12, 18
frio	freddo	frío	cold 12, 19, 23, 29
faculdade	istituto/facoltà	colegio	college 33
comando	comando	orden	command (n) 56
comissão	provvigione	comisión	commission (n) 35, 49
empresa	azienda	empresa	company (n) 7, 28, 32, 34, 46
competição	concorrenza	competencia	competition (n) 35, 45
computador	computer	computadora	computer 7, 17, 42, 45, 46, 56
porteiro	portiere d'albergo	conserje	concierge 11, 13
conferência	congresso	conferencia	conference 8
confirmar	confermare	confirmar	confirm 9
fazer conexão	collegare	conectar	connect 20, 56
contatar	rivolgersi	contactar (con)	contact (v) 25, 46, 60
cópia	copia	copia	copy (n) 36, 52, 56
país	paese	país	country 12, 22, 47, 51
crédito	credito	crédito	credit (n) 25, 40, 50
tripulação	equipaggio	tripulación	crew 55
cruzeiro (n), viajar/passear (v)	crociera (n), fare una crociera (v)	crucero (n), navegar (v)	cruise (n/v) 16, 18, 19, 47, 49, 52, 53
diáriamente	quotidianamente	diario	daily 26
perigoso	pericoloso	peligroso	dangerous 57
dia	giorno	día	day 20, 24, 25, 26, 30, 50, 54
decidir	decidere	decidir	decide 49
diploma	laurea	título	degree 33
entregar	consegnare	entregar	deliver 46, 47
departamento	reparto	departamento	department 17, 27, 31, 34, 42
partida	partenza	salida	departure 1, 3, 51
mesa, escrivaninha	scrivania	escritorio	desk 11, 13, 29, 53
discar	comporre il numero telefonico	discar	dial (v) 34
diferente	diverso	diferente	different 13, 21, 50
direto	diretto/a	directo	direct (adj.) 30, 34
diretor	direttore	director	director 16, 17, 27, 59
discordar	dissentire	discrepar	disagree 34
disco	disco	disco	disc 53, 56
desconto	sconto	descuento	discount (n) 58
descobrir	scoprire	descubrir	discover 57
discutir	discutere	comentar	discuss 9
incomodar	disturbare	perturbar	disturb 15, 34, 42
doutor	dottore	doctor	doctor (n) 16, 27, 31
documento	documento	documento	document 56
dólar	dollaro	dólar	dollar 22, 24, 50
porta	porta	puerta	door 6, 8, 17, 38, 47, 53
bebida (n), beber (v)	bevanda (n), bere (v)	bebida (n), beber (v)	drink (n/v) 2, 19, 28, 48, 56; 42, 55

ENGLISH	FRENCH	JAPANESE	GERMAN
drive (computer) (n) 56	lecteur	ドライブ	Platte
driver 32	conducteur	ドライバー	Fahrer
drop 55	laisser tomber	落ちる	fallenlassen
dry (adj.)12, 23, 47	sec	乾いた	trocken
easy 34	facile	簡単な	leicht
eat 42, 45	manger	食べる	essen
elevator 8	ascenseur	エレベーター	Fahrstuhl
emergency 15	urgence	緊急時	Notfall
empty 39, 51	vide	空の	leer
engineer 29	ingénieur	エンジニア	Ingenieur
enjoy 4, 10, 31, 44, 52, 53, 55, 60	apprécier	楽しむ	genießen
entertainment 17, 26, 53, 59	divertissement	エンターテインメント	Unterhaltung
exchange 15	change	両替	Wechsel-
excursion 16, 17, 26, 31, 55, 57	excursion	小旅行	Ausflug
expect 9, 26	prévoir	期待する	erwarten
expensive 9, 24, 49, 58,	cher	値段が高い	teuer
extension 20, 34, 36	poste	内線	Durchwahl
extra 22, 25, 32, 41, 46	extra	追加の	extra
family 3, 4, 7	famille	家族	Familie
famous 12, 41, 57	fameux	有名な	berühmt
fare (n) 6, 32	tarif	料金	Fahrtkosten
fax 9, 11, 20, 34, 39, 46, 49	fax	ファックス	Fax
file (n) 46	fichier	ファイル	Datei
fill 25, 50	remplir	満たす	füllen
flight 1, 2, 3, 5, 30, 37, 48, 50, 51	vol	フライト	Flug
floor (n) 8, 29	étage	階、床	Etage, Boden
fly 2, 48, 60	voler	飛ぶ	fliegen
follow 6, 13, 34, 36, 46	suivre	従う	folgen
forget 32, 60	oublier	忘れる	vergessen
form (n) 52	formulaire	書式	Formular
free 26, 45, 50, 51	gratuit	空いている	frei
fuel 50	carburant	燃料	Brennstoff
full 7, 23, 25, 30, 50	plein	いっぱい	voll
gallon 50	gallon	ガロン	Gallone
game 42, 45	jeu	ゲーム	Spiel
gas [UK: petrol] 25, 50	essence	ガソリン	Benzin
gate 1, 51	porte	ゲート	Tor
genuine 43, 57, 58	véritable	本物の	echt
glad 31, 37	heureux	嬉しい	froh
gold 57	or	金	Gold
good 23, 31, 33, 37, 44, 55, 59	bon	良い	gut
guess 34, 56	deviner	見当をつける	raten
guest 11, 52	invité	客	Gast
guide (n) 12, 33, 36, 57	guide	ガイド	Führer
half 6, 12	moitié	半分	halb
hall 5	consigne	ホール	Halle
harbor 41, 48	port	港	Hafen
hard 34, 60	difficile	難しい	hart
heavy 5, 6	lourd	重い	schwer

PORTUGUESE	ITALIAN	SPANISH	ENGLISH
drive	unità disco	mecanismo impulsador de discos	drive (computer) (n) 56
motorista	autista	conductor	driver 32
deixar cair	lasciar cadere	dejar caer	drop 55
seco	asciutto/secco	seco	dry (adj.)12, 23, 47
fácil	facile	fácil	easy 34
comer	mangiare	comer	eat 42, 45
elevador	ascensore	ascensor	elevator 8
emergência	emergenza	emergencia	emergency 15
vazio	vuoto	vacío	empty 39, 51
engenheiro	tecnico	ingeniero	engineer 29
apreciar	divertirsi	disfrutar	enjoy 4, 10, 31, 44, 52, 53, 55, 60
divertimento	spettacoli	entretenimiento	entertainment 17, 26, 53, 59
câmbio	cambio	tasa de cambio	exchange 15
excursão	escursione	excursión	excursion 16, 17, 26, 31, 55, 57
esperar	attendere	esperar	expect 9, 26
caro	caro	caro	expensive 9, 24, 49, 58,
ramal	interno	interno	extension 20, 34, 36
extra	supplementare	extra	extra 22, 25, 32, 41, 46
família	famiglia	familia	family 3, 4, 7
famoso	famoso	famoso	famous 12, 41, 57
preço, tarifa	tariffa	precio	fare (n) 6, 32
fax	fax	fax	fax 9, 11, 20, 34, 39, 46, 49
arquivo	file	archivo	file (n) 46
encher	riempire	completar	fill 25, 50
vôo	volo	vuelo	flight 1, 2, 3, 5, 30, 37, 48, 50, 51
andar, chão	piano, pavimento	piso	floor (n) 8, 29
voar	volare	volar	fly 2, 48, 60
seguir	seguire	seguir	follow 6, 13, 34, 36, 46
esquecer	dimenticare	olvidar	forget 32, 60
formulário	modulo	formulario	form (n) 52
livre	libero	libre	free 26, 45, 50, 51
combustível	combustibile; carburante	combustible	fuel 50
cheio	pieno	lleno	full 7, 23, 25, 30, 50
galão	gallone	galón	gallon 50
jogo	gioco	juego	game 42, 45
gasolina	benzina	gasolina	gas [UK: petrol] 25, 50
portão	cancello, uscita (per imbarco)	verja	gate 1, 51
genuíno	genuino	genuino	genuine 43, 57, 58
feliz	lieto	contento	glad 31, 37
ouro	oro	oro	gold 57
bom	bravo; buono	bueno	good 23, 31, 33, 37, 44, 55, 59
adivinhar	indovinare	adivinar	guess 34, 56
hóspede	ospite	invitado	guest 11, 52
guia	guida	guía	guide (n) 12, 33, 36, 57
metade	metà	mitad	half 6, 12
hall	sala (bagagli)	hall de equipaje	hall 5
porto	porto	puerto	harbor 41, 48
difícil	duro	duro	hard 34, 60
pesado	pesante	pesado	heavy 5, 6

ENGLISH	FRENCH	JAPANESE	GERMAN
height 54	hauteur	高さ	Höhe
help (v) 6, 17, 19, 24, 30, 58	aider	助ける	helfen
highway [UK: main road] 57	grand-route	幹線道路	Schnellstraße
hold 8, 20, 47,	tenir	持つ	halten
home 7, 12, 20, 23, 25, 33, 42	foyer	自宅	Heim
hope 31, 52, 53	espérer	希望	hoffen
hot 12, 19, 23, 25	chaud	熱い	heiß
hotel 7, 8, 11, 13, 15, 25, 29. 32, 36, 52, 55, 57	hôtel	ホテル	Hotel
hurry 29, 50, 51	se dépêcher	急ぐ	sich beeilen
idea 6, 42	idée	考え	Idee
immigration 3, 4, 18	immigration	入国	Immigration
important 34, 39, 56, 59	important	重要	wichtig
industry 12	industrie	産業	Industrie
information 11, 20, 34, 40, 46, 53, 56, 58, 59	information	インフォメーション	Informationen
initial (n) 3, (v) 25	initial (n), signer (v)	n=イニシャル、 v=イニシャルを付ける	Anfangsbuchstabe (n), unterzeichnen (v)
inquiry 15, 20, 24, 37	demande de renseignements	問い合わせ	Anfrage
insert (v) 14, 53	insérer	挿入する	einfügen
instruction 14, 34	instruction	指示	Anweisung
insurance 25	assurance	保険	Versicherung
international 1, 5, 6, 11, 18, 24, 40	international	国際的な（の）	international
interrupt 42	interrompre	中断する	unterbrechen
introduce 31, 55	introduire	紹介する	vorstellen
invoice 46	facture	請求書	Rechnung
item 4, 14, 36, 52	article	物品	Gegenstand
janitor [UK: caretaker] 16	gardien	管理人	Hausmeister
job 3, 31, 33, 45, 60	emploi	仕事	Beruf
key (n) 7, 22, 25, 39, 50, 52	clef	鍵	Schlüssel
keyboard 56	clavier	キーボード	Tastatur
knock (v) 56	frapper	ノックする	klopfen
lake 41, 48, 54	lac	湖	See
land (n) 48, 54, 57; (v) 48	terre (n), atterrir (v)	n=土地、v=着陸する	Land (n), landen (v)
laundry 38	linge	洗濯物	Wäsche
lawyer 16	juriste	法律家	Rechtsanwalt
lesson 45	cours	レッスン	Unterrichtsstunde
lever 50	levier	レバー	Hebel
license (n) 7	permis	免許証	Führerschein
list (n) 26, 34, 38, 52	liste	リスト	Liste
listen 36, 45	écouter	聴く	zuhören
live (v) 12, 33	vivre	生きる	leben
lobby 8, 29	hall	ロビー	Lobby
look 17, 19, 20, 49, 55, 58,	regarder	見る	sehen
love 33, 45	aimer	愛（する）	lieben
lucky 23	chanceux	幸運	Glück haben
machine 14, 20, 46	machine	機械	Maschine
mail [UK: post] (n) 9, (v) 11	courrier (n), poster (v)	n=郵便、v=投函する	Post (n), posten (v)
manager 9, 16, 17, 27, 31, 33, 55	manager	部長	Manager

PORTUGUESE	ITALIAN	SPANISH	ENGLISH
altura	altezza	altura	height 54
ajudar	aiutare; assistere	ayudar	help (v) 6, 17, 19, 24, 30, 58
via principal	strada maestra; autostrada	autopista	highway [UK: main road] 57
segurar	tenere	sostener	hold 8, 20, 47,
lar	casa	hogar	home 7, 12, 20, 23, 25, 33, 42
esperar	sperare	esperar	hope 31, 52, 53
quente	caldo	caliente	hot 12, 19, 23, 25
hotel	albergo	hotel	hotel 7, 8, 11, 13, 15, 25, 29. 32, 36, 52, 55, 57
apressar-se	affrettarsi	apuro	hurry 29, 50, 51
idéia	idea	idea	idea 6, 42
imigração	immigrazione	inmigración	immigration 3, 4, 18
importante	importante	importante	important 34, 39, 56, 59
indústria	industria	industria	industry 12
informação	informazioni	información	information 11, 20, 34, 40, 46, 53, 56, 58, 59
inicial (n), rubricar (v)	iniziale (n), siglare (v)	inicial (n), firmar (v)	initial (n) 3, (v) 25
pergunta, informação	domanda	pregunta	inquiry 15, 20, 24, 37
inserir	inserire	insertar	insert (v) 14, 53
instrução	istruzione	instrucción	instruction 14, 34
seguro	assicurazione	seguro	insurance 25
internacional	internazionale	internacional	international 1, 5, 6, 11, 18, 24, 40
interromper	interrompere	interrumpir	interrupt 42
apresentar	introdurre	presentar	introduce 31, 55
fatura	fattura	factura	invoice 46
item	voce	artículo	item 4, 14, 36, 52
zelador	portinaio	portero	janitor [UK: caretaker] 16
emprego	lavoro	empleo	job 3, 31, 33, 45, 60
chave	chiave	llave	key (n) 7, 22, 25, 39, 50, 52
teclado	tastiera	teclado	keyboard 56
bater	bussare	golpear	knock (v) 56
lago	lago	lago	lake 41, 48, 54
terra (n), aterrisar (v)	terra (n); atterrare (v)	tierra (n), aterrizar (v)	land (n) 48, 54, 57; (v) 48
lavanderia	lavanderia	lavadero	laundry 38
advogado	avvocato	abogado	lawyer 16
aula	lezione	clase	lesson 45
alavanca	leva	palanca	lever 50
carteira de motorista	patente	licencia	license (n) 7
lista	elenco	lista	list (n) 26, 34, 38, 52
escutar	ascoltare	escuchar	listen 36, 45
viver	vivere	vivir	live (v) 12, 33
saguão	atrio	sala de recepción	lobby 8, 29
olhar	guardare	mirar	look 17, 19, 20, 49, 55, 58,
adorar	amare	amar	love 33, 45
sortudo	fortunato	afortunado	lucky 23
máquina	macchina	máquina	machine 14, 20, 46
correio (n), enviar por correio (v)	posta (n), impostare (v)	correo (n), enviar por correo (v)	mail [UK: post] (n) 9, (v) 11
gerente	dirigente/responsabile	gerente	manager 9, 16, 17, 27, 31, 33, 55

ENGLISH	FRENCH	JAPANESE	GERMAN
map 11, 13, 25	plan	地図	Landkarte
meet 9, 17, 19, 26, 31, 37, 49, 55, 60	rencontrer	会う	treffen
memory 46 .	mémoire	メモリ	Erinnerung
message 9, 11, 20, 39, 40, 46	message	メッセージ	Nachricht
method 7, 46	méthode	方法	Methode
miss (v) 13, 52	manquer	懐かしく思う	verpassen
mistake 44	erreur	間違い	Fehler
mobile 20	mobile	移動可能な	Handy
modem 20, 46	modem	モデム	Modem
moment 7, 25, 30, 51, 52, 59	instant	瞬間	Augenblick
name 7, 17, 25, 32, 34	nom	名前	Name
need 7, 13, 29, 32, 46, 58	avoir besoin de	必要	brauchen
news 57	nouvelles	ニュース	Nachrichten
newspaper 57	journal	新聞	Zeitung
normal 46, 50	normal	普通の	normal
occupation 3	profession	職業	Beruf
offer (v) 44, 49	offrir	提示する	anbieten
office 9, 17, 24, 35, 37, 49, 55	bureau	オフィス	Büro
operator 15, 34, 40	opérateur	オペレーター	Telefonist
opinion 35, 47	opinion	意見	Meinung
order (v) 44; (n) 46, 47	commander (v), ordre (n)	注文（する）	bestellen (v), Auftrag (n)
pack (v) 51	faire ses bagages	荷造りする	packen
pack 19, 52	sachets	包み	Beutel
packet 19	paquet	小包	Paket
page (n) 35	page	ページ	Seite
paper 39	papier	紙	Papier
party (n) 6	groupe	団体	Gruppe
pass (v) 44	passer	渡す	weiterreichen
passenger 1, 26, 32, 36, 47, 49, 55, 59	passager	旅客	Passagier
passport 3, 4, 7	passeport	パスポート	Paß
pay 7, 21, 25, 28, 32, 50	payer	支払う	zahlen
payment 7, 58	règlement	支払	Zahlung
people 6, 41	gens	人々	Leute
percentage 54	pourcentage	割合	Prozentsatz
permission 32	permission	許可	Erlaubnis
personal 25	personnel	個人的	persönlich
phone (n/v) 20, 34, 39, 40, 46, 49, 59	téléphone (n), téléphoner (v)	電話（する）	Telefon (n), telefonieren (v)
photocopier 46	photocopieuse	コピー機	Fotokopierer
photographer 16, 19, 49, 53, 55, 58	photographe	カメラマン	Fotograf
photo 46	photo	写真	Foto
picture 19, 23, 46, 48, 52, 60	image	写真	Bild
pilot 48	pilote	パイロット	Pilot
place (v) 47; (n) 28, 37	place, placer	v=置く、n=場所	stellen (v), Platz (n)
play (v) 45	jouer	上演する	spielen
please 2, 39, 44, 58	s'il vous plaît	お願いします	bitte
point (n) 25, 54	endroit	点	Punkt
pool 8	piscine	プール	Schwimmbad
population 4, 12, 54, 57	population	人口	Bevölkerung

PORTUGUESE	ITALIAN	SPANISH	ENGLISH
mapa	mappa	mapa	map 11, 13, 25
encontrar	incontrare	encontrarse con	meet 9, 17, 19, 26, 31, 37, 49, 55, 60
memória	memoria	memoria	memory 46
mensagem	messaggio	mensaje	message 9, 11, 20, 39, 40, 46
método	metodo	método	method 7, 46
sentir falta, perder	mancare	extrañar	miss (v) 13, 52
erro	errore	error	mistake 44
móvel	portatile (telefono)	teléfono celular	mobile 20
modem	modem	modem	modem 20, 46
momento	momento	momento	moment 7, 25, 30, 51, 52, 59
nome	nome	nombre	name 7, 17, 25, 32, 34
precisar	avere bisogno di	necesitar	need 7, 13, 29, 32, 46, 58
notícias	notizie	noticias	news 57
jornal	giornale/quotidiano	diario	newspaper 57
normal	normale	normal	normal 46, 50
ocupação	occupazione	ocupación	occupation 3
oferecer	offrire	ofrecer	offer (v) 44, 49
escritório	ufficio	oficina	office 9, 17, 24, 35, 37, 49, 55
operador	operatore	operadora	operator 15, 34, 40
opinião	opinione	opinión	opinion 35, 47
fazer pedido (v), pedido (n)	ordinare (v), ordine (n)	pedir (v), pedido (n)	order (v) 44; (n) 46, 47
empacotar	far le valigie	empacar	pack (v) 51
pacote	sacchetto	paquete	pack 19, 52
pacote	pacchetto	paquete	packet 19
página	pagina	página	page (n) 35
papel	carta	papel	paper 39
grupo	gruppo	fiesta	party (n) 6
passar	passare	pasar	pass (v) 44
passageiro	passeggero	pasajero	passenger 1, 26, 32, 36, 47, 49, 55, 59
passaporte	passaporto	pasaporte	passport 3, 4, 7
pagar	pagare	pagar	pay 7, 21, 25, 28, 32, 50
pagamento	pagamento	pago	payment 7, 58
pessoas	persone	gente	people 6, 41
porcentagem	percentuale	porcentaje	percentage 54
permissão	permesso	permiso	permission 32
pessoal	personale	personal	personal 25
telefone (n), telefonar (v)	telefono (n), telefonare (v)	teléfono (n), telefonear (v)	phone (n/v) 20, 34, 39, 40, 46, 49, 59
fotocopiadora	fotocopiatrice	fotocopiadora	photocopier 46
fotógrafo	fotografo	fotógrafo	photographer 16, 19, 49, 53, 55, 58
fotografia	fotografia	fotografia	photo 46
pintura, desenho, fotografia	quadro	cuadro	picture 19, 23, 46, 48, 52, 60
piloto	pilota	piloto	pilot 48
colocar (v), lugar (n)	posare (v), posto (n)	ubicar (v), lugar (n)	place (v) 47; (n) 28, 37
jogar	giocare	jugar	play (v) 45
por favor	per favore	por favor	please 2, 39, 44, 58
ponto	punto	punto	point (n) 25, 54
piscina	piscina	estanque	pool 8
população	popolazione	población	population 4, 12, 54, 57

ENGLISH	FRENCH	JAPANESE	GERMAN
port 12, 26, 56, 57	port	港	Hafen
postcard 11	carte postale	絵葉書	Postkarte
prefer 20, 34	préférer	〜の方を好む	bevorzugen
press 8, 14, 34, 53	enfoncer	押す	drücken
price 21, 24, 50, 52, 54, 58	tarif	価格	Preis
print (v) 52	imprimer	プリントする	drucken
problem 14, 15, 23, 29, 38, 45, 58	problème	問題	Problem
produce (v) 47	produire	生産する	herstellen
profession 16	profession	専門職	Beruf
program 14, 53, 56	programme	プログラム	Programm
purchase (n) 54	achat	購入する	Kauf
qualification 33	diplôme	資格	Qualifikation
question 31, 50	question	質問	Frage
rate 11	taux	レート	Gebühr, Kurs
reach 5	atteindre	届く	Reichweite
reason 32, 35	raison	理由	Grund
receipt 32, 50	reçu	レシート	Quittung
reception 7, 11, 15	réception	フロント	Rezeption
recommend 10	recommander	推薦する	empfehlen
record (v) 20, 40; (n) 14, 52	enregistrer (v), enregistrement (n)	v=記録する、n=記録	aufnehmen (v), Aufnahme (n)
registration 7	enregistrement	登録	Anmelde (formular)
regular 2, 21, 56	normal	レギュラー	normal, regelmäßig
reject (v) 14	rejeter	拒否する	ablehnen
rental 11, 24, 25	location	レンタル	Miet-
repeat (v) 31	répéter	繰り返す	wiederholen
reply (n) 46	réponse	返事	Antwort
represent 35, 49	représenter	代表する	darstellen
require 34	nécessiter	必要とする	benötigen
reservation 7, 15, 20, 26, 33	réservation	予約	Reservierung
reserve (v) 7, 32	réserver	予約する	reservieren
restroom [UK: public toilet] 17	toilettes	トイレ	öffentliche Toiletten
restaurant 9, 15, 28, 32, 44, 49, 57	restaurant	レストラン	Restaurant
return (v) 25, 42, 60	rapporter	返す	zurückkehren
ride (n) 6, 41, 57	tour	乗ること	Fahrt
road 32	route	道	Straße
room 7, 11, 15, 38, 39, 52,	salle	部屋	Zimmer
route (n) 35	itinéraire	ルート	Strecke
routine 26	routine	日課	Routine
run (v) 29	faire fonctionner	実行する	laufen lassen
sailor 16	marin	船員	Matrose
sales (n) 27	ventes	営業	Verkauf
save 56	sauver	保存する	retten
schedule 41	programme	スケジュール	Zeitplan
seat 1, 17, 19, 30, 50, 51	siège	席	Sitz
secretary 9, 27, 34	secrétaire	秘書	Sekretärin
self-service 28	self-service	セルフサービス	Self-Service
sell (v) 55	vendre	売る	verkaufen
send 29, 46	envoyer	送る	senden
separate 34	séparé	別個の	separat

PORTUGUESE	ITALIAN	SPANISH	ENGLISH
porto	porto	puerto	port 12, 26, 56, 57
cartão postal	cartolina	tarjeta postal	postcard 11
preferir	preferire	preferir	prefer 20, 34
apertar, pressionar	premere	presionar	press 8, 14, 34, 53
preço	prezzo	precio	price 21, 24, 50, 52, 54, 58
imprimir	stampare	imprimir	print (v) 52
problema	problema	problema	problem 14, 15, 23, 29, 38, 45, 58
produzir	produrre	producir	produce (v) 47
profissão	professione	profesión	profession 16
programa	programma	programa	program 14, 53, 56
compra	acquisto	compra	purchase (n) 54
qualificação	qualifica	calificación	qualification 33
pergunta	domanda	pregunta	question 31, 50
taxa	tasso	tasa	rate 11
alcançar	raggiungere	alcanzar	reach 5
razão, motivo	ragione	razón	reason 32, 35
recibo	ricevuta	recibo	receipt 32, 50
recepção	ricevimento	recepción	reception 7, 11, 15
recomendar	raccomandare	recomendar	recommend 10
registrar	registrare (v) voce di registro (n)	registrar (v), registro (n)	record (v) 20, 40; (n) 14, 52
registro	registrazione	tarjeta de inscripción	registration 7
regular	regolare	común, regular	regular 2, 21, 56
rejeitar	respingere	rechazar	reject (v) 14
aluguel	noleggio	alquiler	rental 11, 24, 25
repetir	ripetere	repetir	repeat (v) 31
resposta	risposta	respuesta	reply (n) 46
representar	rappresentare	representar	represent 35, 49
precisar	esigere	requerir	require 34
reserva	prenotazione	reserva	reservation 7, 15, 20, 26, 33
reservar	prenotare	reservar	reserve (v) 7, 32
banheiro público	tolette	aseos sanitarios	restroom [UK: public toilet] 17
restaurante	ristorante	restaurante	restaurant 9, 15, 28, 32, 44, 49, 57
voltar	ritornare	volver	return (v) 25, 42, 60
passeio, viagem	tragitto	paseo	ride (n) 6, 41, 57
rua	strada	camino	road 32
quarto	stanza	cuarto	room 7, 11, 15, 38, 39, 52,
rota	itinerario	ruta	route (n) 35
rotina	routine	rutina	routine 26
correr	correre	correr	run (v) 29
marinheiro	marinaio	marinero	sailor 16
vendas	vendite	ventas	sales (n) 27
salvar	salvare	ahorrar	save 56
horário	programma, tabella oraria	horario	schedule 41
assento	sedile	asiento	seat 1, 17, 19, 30, 50, 51
secretária	segretario/a	secretaria	secretary 9, 27, 34
self-service	self-service	autoservicio	self-service 28
vender	vendere	vender	sell (v) 55
enviar	inviare	enviar	send 29, 46
separar	separato	separar	separate 34

ENGLISH	FRENCH	JAPANESE	GERMAN
server 16, 21	serveur	ウェイター	Kellner, Ober
service (n) 15, 38, 40, 53	service	サービス	Dienstleistungen
set 28	fixe	セット	Tagesmenu, Tageskarte
shake (v) 8	serrer	握手する	schütteln
share (v) 6	partager	共有する	teilen
ship (n) 16, 17, 26, 31, 33, 36, 37, 41, 49; (v) 58	navire (n), transporter (v)	n=船、v=送付する	Schiff (n), versenden (v)
shop (n) 58	boutique	店	Geschäft
shout (v) 46	crier	叫ぶ	rufen
sightseeing 36, 52, 57	faire du tourisme	観光	Besichtigungstour
sign (n) 6, 13, 22, 25, 52	signe	看板	Schild
similar 26, 31	similaire	似た	ähnlich
simple 46	simple	単純な	einfach
single 7	simple	シングル	einzeln
sit 32, 53	s'asseoir	すわる	sitzen
size 22, 54	taille	サイズ	Größe
snow (n) 57	neige	雪	Schnee
sorry 1, 2, 21, 35, 39, 42, 44, 59	désolé	残念に思う	Entschuldigung!
souvenir 57	souvenir	おみやげ	Souvenir
space 58	espace	空間	Raum
special 24, 47	spécial	特別な	besonders
specialty 24	spécialité	スペシャリティ	Spezialität
sport 17, 27, 33, 40, 42, 45, 53, 56	sport	スポーツ	Sport
stairs 17	escaliers	階段	Treppe
stamp (n) 29, 50	timbre	切手	Briefmarke
stand (v) 4, 5, 51	se tenir debout	立つ	stehen
start (v) 14, 44, 56	démarrer	始める	starten
station 13, 50	gare	駅	Bahnhof
stay 4, 9, 23, 48, 49, 52	rester	滞在する	Aufenthalt
step (v) 4	marcher	ステップする	treten
stop (v) 29, 30, 34	arrêter	止まる	halten
store (n) 8, 22, 57	magasin	店	Geschäft
strange 55	étrange	変わった	eigenartig
street 7, 8, 13, 28, 32	rue	通り	Straße
structure (n) 27	structure	構造	Aufbau
suggest 60	suggérer	示唆する	vorschlagen
suit (v) 30	convenir	合う	passen
superior 27, 31	supérieur	上位の	besser
supermarket 30, 39	supermarché	スーパーマーケット	Supermarkt
surprise (n) 60	surprise	驚き	Überraschung
switchboard 34	standard téléphonique	電話オペレーター	Vermittlung
table 9, 10, 32, 53	table	テーブル	Tisch
take off (v) 48	décoller	離陸する	starten
tank 25, 50	réservoir	タンク	Tank
tax 21, 22	taxe	税金	Steuer
taxi (v) 48	rouler lentement	飛行機をタクシングする	ausrollen
taxi (n) 6, 13, 16, 32, 48	taxi	タクシー	Taxi
tea 2, 10, 19, 21, 23, 28	thé	お茶	Tee
team 26	équipe	チーム	Team
telephone 20, 25, 40, 46, 53	téléphone	電話	Telefon
tennis 9, 33, 45	tennis	テニス	Tennis

PORTUGUESE	ITALIAN	SPANISH	ENGLISH
garçom	cameriere	camarero	server 16, 21
serviço	servizio	servicio	service (n) 15, 38, 40, 53
fixo (as in 'menu fixo'.)	fisso	fijo	set 28
dar a mão	stringere (la mano)	estrechar (la mano)	shake (v) 8
repartir	condividere	compartir	share (v) 6
navio (n), enviar por navio (v)	nave (n), spedire (v) (via mare)	barco (n), fletar (v)	ship (n) 16, 17, 26, 31, 33, 36, 37, 41, 49; (v) 58
loja	negozio	tienda	shop (n) 58
gritar	gridare	gritar	shout (v) 46
passeio turístico	gita	visita de puntos de interés	sightseeing 36, 52, 57
placa, sinal	segnaletica stradale	cartel	sign (n) 6, 13, 22, 25, 52
similar	simile	similar	similar 26, 31
simples	semplice	simple	simple 46
(quarto de) solteiro	singolo	único	single 7
sentar-se	sedere	sentar(se)	sit 32, 53
tamanho	misura	tamaño	size 22, 54
neve	neve	nieve	snow (n) 57
desculpe-me	scusi	perdón	sorry 1, 2, 21, 35, 39, 42, 44, 59
souvenir	souvenir	recuerdo	souvenir 57
espaço	spazio	espacio	space 58
especial	speciale	especial	special 24, 47
especialidade	specialità	especialidad	specialty 24
esporte	sport	deporte	sport 17, 27, 33, 40, 42, 45, 53, 56
escada	scale	escalera	stairs 17
selo	francobollo	estampilla	stamp (n) 29, 50
ficar (em pé)	stare in piedi	parar(se)	stand (v) 4, 5, 51
começar	iniziare	comenzar	start (v) 14, 44, 56
estação	stazione	estación	station 13, 50
estadia	soggiorno	permanecer	stay 4, 9, 23, 48, 49, 52
dar um passo	camminare	salir	step (v) 4
parar	fermare	terminar	stop (v) 29, 30, 34
loja	negozio	tienda	store (n) 8, 22, 57
estranho	strano	extraño	strange 55
rua	strada	calle	street 7, 8, 13, 28, 32
estrutura	struttura	estructura	structure (n) 27
sugerir	suggerire	sugerir	suggest 60
servir	vestito	ajustar	suit (v) 30
superior	superiore	superior	superior 27, 31
supermercado	supermercato	supermercado	supermarket 30, 39
surpresa	sorpresa	sorpresa	surprise (n) 60
PABX	centralino	conmutador	switchboard 34
mesa	tavolo	mesa	table 9, 10, 32, 53
decolar	decollare	despegar	take off (v) 48
tanque	serbatoio	tanque	tank 25, 50
imposto	tassa	impuesto	tax 21, 22
movimentar-se por terra	rullare (aereo)	carretear	taxi (v) 48
taxi	tassì	taxi	taxi (n) 6, 13, 16, 32, 48
chá	tè	té	tea 2, 10, 19, 21, 23, 28
equipe, time	squadra	equipo	team 26
telefone	telefono	teléfono	telephone 20, 25, 40, 46, 53
tênis	tennis	tenis	tennis 9, 33, 45

ENGLISH	FRENCH	JAPANESE	GERMAN
terminal 6, 12, 13, 30	terminus	ターミナル	Terminal
theater 13, 16, 17, 26, 45	théâtre	劇場	Theater
think 23, 32, 42	penser	考える	denken
ticket 51	ticket	チケット	Karte
total 52	total	合計	insgesamt
touch 60	toucher	触れる	berühren
tour 7, 16, 31, 33, 36	visite	ツアー	Tour
tourist 6, 57	touriste	観光客	Tourist
town 23, 30, 49, 57	ville	町	Stadt
travel (v) 4, 6, 26, 48, 53	voyager	旅行	reisen
trip 11, 16, 48, 55	voyage	旅行	Reise
try 7, 20, 42, 47	essayer	試す	versuchen
turn 13, 33, 56	tourner	回る	drehen
understand 2, 6	comprendre	理解する	verstehen
urgent 29, 34, 46	urgent	急ぎの	dringend
use (v) 31, 56	utiliser	使う	nutzen
vacation [UK: holiday] 3, 11, 16, 37, 49	congés	休暇	Urlaub
valet 15, 38	valet	ベルボーイ	Kammerdiener
valley 48	vallée	谷	Tal
vegetarian 2, 43	végétarien	ベジタリアン	Vegetarier
vehicle 24, 57	véhicule	車両	Fahrzeug
video 20, 49, 53	vidéo	ビデオ	Video
visa 3	visa	ビザ	Visum
visit (n) 23, 37, 57	visite	訪問	Besuch
voucher 50	bon	クーポン券	Gutschein
wait 8, 9, 19, 20, 32, 46, 51	attendre	待つ	warten
waiter 10	serveur	ウェイター	Kellner, Ober
walk (n) 4, 13	promenade	散歩	Spaziergang
walk (v) 13, 48	marcher	歩く	laufen
want 7, 15, 23, 24, 25, 31, 35, 46, 47, 52	vouloir	欲しい	mögen
warm 44	tiède	暖かい	warm
waste (v) 47	gaspiller	無駄にする	vergeuden
watch (v) 45, 53	regarder	見る	beobachten
water (n) 2, 12, 29, 42, 44	eau	水	Wasser
way 13, 23	voie	道	Weg
weather 8, 23, 41, 55	temps	天気	Wetter
wet (adj) 12, 23	humide	濡れた	naß
window 1, 51, 53, 56	fenêtre	窓	Fenster
work (v) 14, 16, 17, 31, 34, 45, 50, 53, 60	travailler	仕事	arbeiten
world 12, 16, 57	monde	世界	Welt
worry 5, 14, 29	s'inquiéter	心配	sich sorgen
write 34	écrire	書く	schreiben
wrong 15, 50	faux	間違った	falsch
zip code [UK: postcode] 7	code postal	郵便番号	Postleitzahl
zoo 12	zoo	動物園	Zoo

PORTUGUESE	ITALIAN	SPANISH	ENGLISH
terminal	terminal	terminal	terminal 6, 12, 13, 30
teatro	teatro	teatro	theater 13, 16, 17, 26, 45
pensar	pensare	pensar	think 23, 32, 42
passagem, entrada	biglietto	pasaje	ticket 51
total	totale	total	total 52
tocar	tocco	tocar	touch 60
tour	gita turistica	excursión	tour 7, 16, 31, 33, 36
turista	turista	turista	tourist 6, 57
cidade	città	ciudad	town 23, 30, 49, 57
viajar	viaggiare	viajar	travel (v) 4, 6, 26, 48, 53
ciagem	viaggio	viaje	trip 11, 16, 48, 55
tentar	cercare	intentar	try 7, 20, 42, 47
virar-se	girare	turno	turn 13, 33, 56
compreender	capire	comprender	understand 2, 6
urgente	urgente	urgente	urgent 29, 34, 46
usar	utilizzare	usar	use (v) 31, 56
férias	vacanza	vacaciones	vacation [UK: holiday] 3, 11, 16, 37, 49
camareiro	cameriere	valet	valet 15, 38
vale	valle	valle	valley 48
vegetariano	vegetariano	vegetariano	vegetarian 2, 43
veículo	veicolo	vehículo	vehicle 24, 57
vídeo	video	video	video 20, 49, 53
visto	visto	visa	visa 3
visita	visita	visita	visit (n) 23, 37, 57
vale	buono	cupón	voucher 50
esperar	attendere	esperar	wait 8, 9, 19, 20, 32, 46, 51
garçom	cameriere	camarero	waiter 10
caminhada	passeggiata	caminata	walk (n) 4, 13
andar	camminare	caminar	walk (v) 13, 48
querer	volere	querer	want 7, 15, 23, 24, 25, 31, 35, 46, 47, 52
morno	caldo	cálido	warm 44
perder (tempo)	sprecare	desperdiciar	waste (v) 47
observar	osservare	mirar	watch (v) 45, 53
água	acqua (n)	agua	water (n) 2, 12, 29, 42, 44
direção, caminho	via	camino	way 13, 23
clima	tempo	tiempo	weather 8, 23, 41, 55
molhado	bagnato (a)	mojado	wet (adj) 12, 23
janela	finestra	ventana	window 1, 51, 53, 56
trabalhar	lavorare	trabajar	work (v) 14, 16, 17, 31, 34, 45, 50, 53, 60
mundo	mondo	mundo	world 12, 16, 57
preocupar-se	preoccuparsi	preocupar(se)	worry 5, 14, 29
escrever	scrivere	escribir	write 34
errado	sbagliato	equivocado	wrong 15, 50
código postal	codice postale	código postal	zip code [UK: postcode] 7
zoológico	zoo	jardín zoológico	zoo 12

Macmillan Heinemann English Language Teaching

Between Towns Road, Oxford OX4 3PP, UK

A division of Macmillan Publishers Limited

Companies and representatives throughout the world

Text © Peter Viney 1996

Design and illustration © Macmillan Publishers Limited 1998

Heinemann is a registered trademark of Reed Educational & Professional Publishing Limited

First published 1996

Survival Files based on concept by Anne Watson Delestrée
Additional material written by Anne Watson Delestrée

Designed by Shireen Nathoo Design
Commissioned photography by Sue Baker (9, 11, 28 b, 35, 36, 44, 51); Chris Honeywell (3, 5, 7, 10, 14, 15, 16, 17, 19, 21, 22, 23, 25, 26, 27, 28 t, 29 main, t, b, l, 30 l, 31, 33, 37, 38, 39, 42, 47, 49, 52, 55, 56, 59, 60).
Illustrations by: Richard Draper (topic symbols, introduction artwork, 5, 13); Tim Slade (2, 15, 16, 19, 21, 43, 49, 54, 58); Jerry Fowler (8, 46, 53).

Cover design by Shireen Nathoo Design
Cover photography by Tony Stone Images - Bruce Ayres; Chris Honeywell

Student's Book (Asian ed)	ISBN 0 435 29682 5
Student's Book (Int ed)	ISBN 0 435 29688 4
Teacher's File	ISBN 0 435 29684 1
Practice Book	ISBN 0 435 29683 3
Audio Cassettes	ISBN 0 435 29685 X
Audio CDs	ISBN 0 435 29686 8

The author would like to thank his editors at Heinemann, Betina Cochran, Denise Cripps and Clare Leeds, for their enthusiasm, hard work and creative input on Basic Survival.

The publishers would like to thank Terry Ringe of Agency 2, Avis, Gabrielle Davis of Barbizon, Denny's, Mark Dudley, Vicki Durham of Old Town Travel and Tours, Gordon Harkins, Abbey Trybulski and Brad Logstin of Hilton Beach and Tennis Resort, Erin Frye of Hornblower Dining Yachts, Marcia D Rebello, Nancy Manas of San Diego Visitors and Convention Centre, Simon Stanford, Valerie of Super 8 Motel - El Cajon, Nino of Trattoria Fantastica.

The authors and publishers would like to thank the following for permission to reproduce their material: Richard Bryant/Arcaid (8); Robert Estall (41 t, r); The Image Bank (4, 18, 20 t); Interfoto (34); Micheal Dent/Impact (13 b), Impact (48); Photonica (32); The Photographers Library (41 t, m); Quadrant Picture Library (24); Rex Features (6); Tony Stone Images (1, 12, 20 b, 30 r, 35, 40, 50, 54, 57 b, r); SuperStock (13 t & m, 41 t, l & b, 45); Trip (2); Peter Viney (57 b, l & t, 58); Zefa (29 b, r).

Printed in China

2004 2003 2002 2001
13 12 11 10 9 8 7 6